MARY BERRY is well known as the author of more than thirty very popular cookery books, including her earlier *AGA Cookbook*, *The Complete Cookbook*, *Mary Berry Cooks Cakes*, *The New Cook* and *Cook Now, Eat Later*. She has presented several television cookery series – notably 'Mary Berry at Home' and 'Mary Berry's Ultimate Cakes' – and contributed to radio programmes and cookery magazines. She is loved for her practical and unfussy approach to preparing and serving food and is recognised as the queen of Aga cookery. She runs Aga workshops from her home in Buckinghamshire where she also works in her beautiful garden, her other great passion.

MARY BERRY'S NEW AGA COOKBOOK

MARY BERRY

headline

Recent books by Mary Berry

The New Cook
Mary Berry Cooks Puddings and Desserts
Mary Berry Cooks Cakes
Mary Berry at Home
The Complete Cookbook
The Ultimate Cake Book
Quick and Easy Cake Book
Cook Now, Eat Later

First published in 1999
by HEADLINE BOOK PUBLISHING

First published in paperback in 2003
by HEADLINE BOOK PUBLISHING

10 9 8 7 6 5 4 3 2 1

Cataloguing in Publication Data is available from the British Library

ISBN 0 7472 7358 8

Photographs by James Murphy
Edited by Susan Fleming
Designed by Isobel Gillan
Typeset by Letterpart Limited, Reigate, Surrey

Printed and bound in Great Britain by
Butler and Tanner Ltd

HEADLINE BOOK PUBLISHING
A division of Hodder Headline
338 Euston Road
London NW1 3BH

www.headline.co.uk
www.hodderheadline.com

CONTENTS

ACKNOWLEDGEMENTS

For the past ten years I have been running Aga workshops from my home in Penn, Buckinghamshire. Lucy Young, my assistant for almost all of those ten years, has masterminded every day and every course with unfaltering enthusiasm, and has given much painstaking care to every detail concerning all our recipes for books and television. She has spurred me on to write this book, which contains the best new and most popular recipes from our workshops. Thank you, Lucy, for your friendship and unfailing support.

Over the years I have had inspiration and help with these Aga recipes from Izzie Forrest, Sheila Inglis and Penny Tetley. It was actually Penny's mother's Aga that I first cooked on years ago.

This is the sixth book I have worked on with Fiona Oyston. She has tested the recipes for electric and gas temperatures too, just in case you haven't an Aga. Fiona and Peter now have two lovely boys, so it has been quite a challenge for her!

Susan Fleming has worked with me on many books too, and again has converted my jottings into legible text with no spelling mistakes. Although Susan doesn't have an Aga, she enjoys being a 'Sue-chef' on a friend's Aga in Suffolk.

Aga-Rayburn have supported me in every way, keeping me up to date with the latest developments so that I can pass on news of any slight modifications as they occur. I have so often called upon Hazel Jordan, Dawn Roads and, recently, Andy Vaughan. I thank them all.

My editor, Heather Holden-Brown, is special and remarkable. She has been to so much effort to see that this book contains what I feel Aga owners want – simple, inspirational recipes that don't take an age to make, recipes that family and friends are going to enthuse over and ask for again and again. If the phone rang at 6.30 or 7 pm when I was writing this book, it would be Heather dotting the i's and crossing the t's. The book has clear, beautiful photographs too, using pans and trays kindly supplied by Berndes, ICTC and Kuhn Rikon. Thank you to Heather, to Celia Kent and the Headline team.

Thank you too, to a close friend, Jilly Bull, for letting me be photographed for the cover of this book in her glamorous kitchen. The attractive tiles at the back of her Aga come from Jan Harmer of Tile Art in Burford, Oxfordshire.

And last but by no means least, thank you to my family. Paul, my lovely husband, Tom, Sarah and Annabel have all shared the joy when dishes go well, and are full of exciting suggestions for new things to try in the Aga.

INTRODUCTION

I have been happily living with an Aga now for more years than I care to remember. As I've said so many times before – in my books, television programmes and Aga workshops – an Aga rapidly becomes the centre attraction of the kitchen, acting as a warm focus for family, friends and animals. And cooking on an Aga is still a daily joy for me: its spacious ovens produce perfectly cooked dishes, time after time. Even the *look* of the Aga gives me pleasure: I love its smart appearance and gleaming hotplate lids.

It is fifteen years since I wrote *The Aga Book*, commissioned by Aga-Rayburn. A copy of this goes out with every new Aga, and I know, from a mass of letters and conversations, that it is invaluable to all new Aga owners. Long may it continue to be the Aga Bible, and I have written this new book not to supersede it but to complement it. There have been many new trends in cooking in the intervening years, and a plethora of new ingredients, and it is these that I have explored in the recipes here, adapting many ideas to the Aga way of cooking. (I haven't forgotten those who still cook on conventional cookers, though, and give them instructions on each recipe.)

I hope you will enjoy reading and trying out many of the following dishes. We have had fun inventing and testing them! Most are new and up-to-date – although a few will be familiar (adapted old favourites, which I just couldn't bear to leave out) – and are cooked to perfection in the Aga, showing how versatile it really is. Once again, too, this is a book that I have really enjoyed working on – for writing about my Aga is like writing about one of my oldest friends.

MARY BERRY

GETTING TO KNOW YOUR AGA

An Aga is a range cooker, made of cast iron, which is designed to store heat. This is obviously beneficial so far as cooking is concerned, but it also means the kitchen is constantly warm and welcoming, one of the major perceived benefits of range cookers.

Agas are larger than conventional cookers, with more oven space, and can be run on a variety of fuels – electricity, gas (natural and propane), oil and solid fuel. They can be sited in a wide number of places, and now with the introduction of the Aga gas power flue, many can even be fitted on inside walls, no longer requiring a chimney or access to an outside wall.

CHOOSING AN AGA

What you choose will depend on a number of factors – the fuel on offer where you live, the space available in your kitchen, the size of your family, and how much cooking you like to do. And obviously choosing your favourite colour too!

▮ *Two-oven Agas*

A two-oven Aga is suitable for most kitchens. With two ovens and two hotplates, it can cope with most families' cooking demands. My friend Penny loves entertaining, and regularly has twelve people for lunch – all on a reconditioned two-oven Aga, bought from her local Aga Shop. It just takes organisation, and of course the ovens are so much more roomy than conventional ovens. I find that of the people who come to my Aga workshops, some 70 per cent have two-oven Agas.

The Roasting Oven is at the top, the Simmering Oven below. The Boiling Plate is on the left on top, the Simmering Plate to the right.

▮▮ *Four-oven Agas*

This will be the choice of a larger family or those who cook and entertain on a larger scale. I'm devoted to mine, but then I cook a lot for my family and friends, as well as demonstrate at Aga workshops and test recipes for my books and television programmes.

The Roasting Oven is top right, the Baking Oven bottom right, the Simmering Oven top left and the Warming Oven bottom left. The Boiling Plate is to the left on top, the Simmering Plate to the right. There is also a Warming Plate to the left of the hotplates, useful for warming the teapot or sauceboats, or for resting the roast after it has been taken from the oven.

The Aga Module and Companion

Both Module and Companion offer the back-up benefits of conventional cooking, and look as stylish as the Aga. They might appeal particularly to two-oven Aga owners who regret not having a four-oven Aga and want extra space.

The Module

This is an additional cooker which is attached to the left-hand side of either a traditional two-oven or four-oven Aga. It has two electrically heated ovens (one conventional, one fanned), a grill, and a ceramic hob with four rapid-response heat zones, or you can have a four-burner gas hob.

TWO-OVEN AGA

FOUR-OVEN AGA

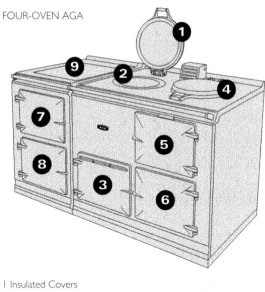

1 Insulated Covers	4 Simmering Plate
2 Boiling Plate	5 Roasting Oven
3 Heat source	6 Simmering Oven

1 Insulated Covers	
2 Boiling Plate	6 Baking Oven
3 Heat source	7 Simmering Oven
4 Simmering Plate	8 Warming Oven
5 Roasting Oven	9 Warming Plate

The Companion

This is like the Module, but free standing and it can be sited anywhere in the kitchen. Its height is that of standard kitchen units.

New or Old?

I would always go for a new Aga, because although Aga cookers don't wear out and can last a lifetime – the company has been going now for over 60 years – new Agas are very much more advanced. If you inherit an Aga with the house you are buying, it will work well but, because it might be older, it will work *differently* from a new Aga. (Have it serviced before you move in, if possible.) The Simmering Oven in older Agas, for instance, is very much slower than in new Agas, as is the Simmering Plate. You used to be able to make any type of porridge overnight in an old Simmering Oven. In a modern Aga, you can only do

Right: The Companion with four gas burners. If preferred, you can have a ceramic hob.

this if you use Scottish pinhead oats (see recipe page 20). Similarly, a lot of people who've had an Aga for years get quite a shock when they buy a new one, because of the marked difference in the simmering times. When I do Aga workshops, Penny – who has an older two-oven Aga – often helps me (and is a great asset). If I say a casserole will take me about 3 hours, Penny will affirm that in her oven it will take up to double that. It's just a case of getting used to your own individual cooker – they're all different.

A Reconditioned Aga

This is an Aga which you will buy second-hand rather than new. It should have been stripped down and rebuilt, to be used as new. Only if this service has been done by properly trained Aga personnel, will Aga recommend the purchase of reconditioned Agas.

Reconditioned Agas could be quite old, which means that they may operate less swiftly than new Agas (see above). Reconditioning should not change the operating temperature or efficiency of the Aga.

A Converted Aga

When described as converted, an Aga has been adapted in order to alter the type of fuel used – from solid fuel to oil, for instance. Aga are not very keen on the purchase of such appliances, unless they have been converted by their specialists, as each original cooker was specially designed to utilise the original type of fuel, and many problems, some of them actually dangerous, can ensue. Having said that, a properly converted Aga can be as good as any other Aga.

Which Fuel?

This will depend on what is available in your home or locality. Gas, for instance, might not be piped to a village in the heart of the country. Oil is currently the cheapest fuel, but you will need to house a storage tank. Solid fuel appliances have to be emptied and refuelled, and you will need space to store the fuel itself. Electric appliances are probably the most economical to run because they can take advantage of cheap-rate electricity. Aga can arrange for a Home Survey Manager to visit your kitchen and give you free advice, which is well worth taking advantage of.

Is an Aga More Expensive to Run?

This is a question often asked, because of course Agas are switched on all the time. I can't honestly say that I have ever done the equation, so I can't swear that it is more or less expensive than a conventional cooker. You can get approximate costs from your Aga Cooker Centre or Aga Shop.

What I can say, though, is that I think our house would be very miserable without the Aga in the months like May when we have our central heating off. That end of the house is aired on damp days, and I can do the 'ironing' of some things I am not so fussy about, like aprons and tea-towels, on the Aga. Because you have an Aga, and it is nice and warm, your kitchen becomes the family room: the children want to do their homework there, my husband likes to frame or clean a picture there, the dogs are always milling around. The Aga becomes the centre of the house, and so enriches family life. Therefore if it costs a bit more, it is worth it!

Can the Heat Be Regulated?

Many new Aga owners panic when they realise that the cooker heat appears not to be so controllable as in conventional cookers. But the constant heat will work in the cook's favour, and exact temperatures will become less important as he or she becomes used to the Aga. The temperature of the Aga should be checked every morning, and if the mercury on the heat indicator is at the single black line, the Aga has its full amount of stored heat.

Aga cookers do actually have thermostats, though, and many Aga owners turn their cookers down slightly in the summer, particularly if they have a smaller kitchen which can get quite warm. However, if you don't like a warm kitchen you won't have a hot oven. You must remember that it will work more slowly with the heat turned down, and recipes will take longer to cook. A lot of people also turn their Agas up slightly at Christmas, or when they're doing a lot of entertaining. In either case, don't forget to put the thermostat back to normal afterwards.

INSTALLING YOUR AGA

Obviously the actual installation of a new Aga from scratch will be done by specialist Aga engineers. But do think carefully beforehand about where the Aga should go in your kitchen, and design the rest of the kitchen around it if possible.

I have owned a number of Agas over the years, and now know exactly what I like and need.

Where to Put Your Aga in the Kitchen

• First, you don't always need to site an Aga on an outside wall; the Aga gas power flue and electric models can be placed on an inside wall. Gas Aga cookers are the most amenable to being sited anywhere. A home survey to assess the technical aspects of installing your Aga is offered by the Aga retailer and is a must to ensure suitability for your kitchen.

• Don't let your Aga sit as an island in the middle of your wall. Think about when you have a big pan of stock, your roast potatoes or turkey – where are you going to put them when you lift them out of the oven? You need surfaces on one side at least, preferably both sides, and these should be of a material suitable to take hot dishes.

• Build units right up to the side of the Aga, as you don't want any space where dirt and grease can gather.

• The Aga should not be too far from the sink. When we had our kitchen built, the one thing that I meant to put in, and forgot, was a tap behind the Aga (the water pipes go along the wall). If I had put this in to fill the kettle, etc., it would have made things easier.

Tiling

It is essential to put tiles behind your Aga, as they are so easy to clean. Match them to your Aga. Don't choose a very bright colour tile or too bold a design, as you may get fed up with it. A kitchen with an Aga is a room the family spends most time in, so it's a good idea to choose something restful. Do not tile down on to the top plate, but behind.

Shelving

You can put shelves either side of the Aga on which you could store things like salt, pepper, sugar, flour or coffee. If the space were deep enough, you could put a tiled shelf at the back where you could store pans.

Drying/Airing

If you have a rail with hanging hooks above the Aga, you could suspend kitchen utensils from it. They would look good, and it's a good way of drying those awkward things like graters which can rust if damp for too long. Useful, too, for airing shirts on hangers.

Storage

It's also very important to have storage space at the side of the Aga, beneath the working surface. This is for pots, pans, shelves (grid and plain) and even the Aga toaster. A narrow vertical open space is best for the oven shelves and roasting tins, as you can identify and reach them quickly and easily (see below).

EQUIPMENT FOR YOUR AGA

When your new Aga is delivered, it will come complete with some free equipment: two oven grid shelves; a plain oven shelf; two roasting tins, one large and one small, each with a suitably sized grill rack; a wire brush; and the Aga toaster, plus *The Aga Book* which I wrote.

Extra equipment can be obtained from your Aga Cooker Centre or Aga Shop.

The Grid Shelves

These are designed to slot into and along the runners on the sides of the Roasting, Baking and Simmering Ovens. There are non-tilt lugs near the front of the oven (to stop trays tilting too far), and the grid shelves themselves are designed so that they cannot easily come right out when pulled forward. You can also place them on the floor of the ovens to prevent your dish from getting too brown underneath.

The Plain Shelf

The plain shelf fits all the ovens, and can be used as a baking sheet for baking pizzas, rolls or scones. Its main use, however, is as a 'cold sheet'. It should be inserted cold, on the second or third set of runners from the top of the Roasting Oven, to prevent the food below – say, a crumble – becoming too scorched or brown on top. It moderates and reduces the heat from the top. This is only effective, however, if the sheet is cold: after 20 minutes or so in the oven, it will have absorbed a lot of heat. Take the shelf out periodically and run cold water over to reduce its temperature – or pop it outside the back door, where it will cool down quickly.

The Roasting Tins

These can be used on the runners or on the floor of the ovens, the large lengthways, the smaller widthways. They are obviously perfect for roasts, but I also use them for traybake cakes and things like moussaka and lasagne. They are handy for holding dishes that might spill over, such as fruit pies. I think it is a good idea to buy an extra small roasting tin so that you roast the joint and potatoes in separate tins at the same time, side by side – this enables you to turn the potatoes without bringing out the roast. The large tin can also be used as you might the plain shelf (see above) when baking small cakes, etc., on the plain shelf.

The Grill Racks

These are reversible, to be used in two positions in the roasting tins. When standing proud of the tin, the rack is good for grilling bacon, chops, etc., at the top of the Roasting Oven. When it is reversed, so that it is sitting *in* the tin, the rack can be used for roasting, keeping meats and poultry out of the fat in the pan. They can be used as a cooling rack, for cakes and breads, etc.

The Wire Brush

This is for cleaning purposes (see page 15).

The Toaster

The circular wire-mesh toaster is surprisingly efficient. The same size as the hotplates, it holds up to four slices of bread between the two frames. Placed on the hotplate and the lid closed, it toasts within minutes. Do not grease the toaster, or wash it. The intense heat will keep it clean. Remember always to preheat it.

Pans and Cookware

Aga do not supply pans with a new Aga, but they make a wonderful range that has been designed specifically for the Aga. Speak to your Aga specialist or read the Aga magazine. The pans are strong, durable, stack beautifully in and out of the Aga, and will last you a lifetime.

Which Pans Are Suitable?

Before splashing out, look at your own pans first. Good quality stainless-steel pans conduct heat most efficiently. Aluminium pans are very good, as are some types of non-stick. They must all be heavy-duty, though, with a strong, thick base. To test their suitability for the Aga, fill each pan with water and place on the Boiling Plate. Put your hands either side and if the pan is rocking, it is not making a good enough contact with the plate – and this is a waste of time and money. The base must be completely level.

Pans should also be wide rather than deep, as these will use the heat from the hotplates more efficiently. For the same reason, a wok with a small base is not very suitable for the Aga as too much heat is lost; it's much better to use a wide frying pan for stir-frying.

Many other pans you may already possess can be used in the Aga. Heavy cast-iron or stainless-steel dishes and casseroles are very good: they can go on the top, and then in the ovens. I find non-stick grill pans (some with lids) very useful; you can use them on the top of the Aga, or on the floor of the Roasting Oven. They are vital for browning something like fish. My grill pans and frying pans all have removable handles so that they can go in the oven. Oblong lasagne dishes can fit in the Roasting Oven one behind the other – fish pie in one perhaps, bread and butter pudding in the other. You can use cast-iron, enamel, ceramic or glass in the ovens, but the latter two cannot be used on the two hotplates.

My Favourite Pans

I have some tried and tested pans which I use all the time because I know they will give me perfect results. These are pictured below.

Clockwise from centre top: 5 litre stainless-steel Aga stewpot and 2 litre stainless-steel Aga low casserole; 28cm Berndes sauté pan with removable handle and glass lid; 20cm Berndes frypan with removable handle on top of 26cm Berndes square ribbed grill pan with removable handle; 1.5 litre stainless-steel Aga saucepan; 10 litre stainless-steel Aga preserving pan (Aga stainless steel supplied by Kuhn Rikon; Berndes supplied by ICTC.)

Use the Boiling Plate for fast boiling or stir-frying.

The Kettle

It is sensible to buy a kettle for the Aga. There are some very snazzy ones in the shops which won't have the thick level base necessary, and although they look good, don't boil very fast. Choose one that is the right size for the amount of water you usually boil. A good kettle on an Aga can actually boil faster than many other kettles, because the heat of the Boiling Plate is so constant and immediate.

The Aga Cake Baker

One thing is particularly useful for those of you who love baking and have a two-oven Aga which lacks a Baking Oven. Aga sell a cake baker which is a pan with a flat lid. Like a Dutch oven, it comes with a rack and three cake tins. First, the empty cake baker is preheated on the floor of the Roasting Oven. Then the raw cake mixture goes in the selected cake tin on the rack in the hot baker. The lid is put on and the

baker put back on the floor of the Roasting Oven where it bakes in a newly created moderate heat absorbed from the high heat of the Roasting Oven. Most cakes take about an hour.

Lift-Off

I use a lot of Lift-Off (also sometimes called Magic Paper) on baking sheets in the Aga. This is non-stick graphite material which is very durable (I've been using some pieces for about thirteen years now!). In some cases you have to grease it, but on the whole for meringues, pizzas, fish fingers, etc., you don't have to. It makes washing-up very much easier, and is healthier than greasing a baking sheet. The Aga Cooker Centres and Aga Shops sell a very good, thinner version called Bac-O-Glide.

LOOKING AFTER YOUR AGA

One of the nicest things about the Aga is that there is so little cleaning to be done. For new owners who have used conventional ovens in the past, this comes as a very pleasant surprise. However, the best way to keep your Aga clean is not to let it get dirty in the first place. Wiping with a damp cloth as you go along, every time you use the Aga, will keep it looking good and prevent any potential build-up of grease or dirt. If you make this a habit, you should never have too much of a problem.

Cleaning

Outside of the Aga: Top, Front and Doors

If stains do appear, the best product to use is Astonish, a good all-round, non-abrasive cleaner sold in the Aga outlets, and by selected mail-order companies. Just put it on and wipe it off. Gentle proprietory cream cleaners can be used as well. Should the enamel on the top be very dirty you can use a caustic cleaner with great care. Wear rubber gloves and carefully avoid the metal strip on the left of the Boiling Plate on some four-oven Agas, and keep away from the temperature gauge.

I love the glossy enamel top of my Aga and am very careful with it. I try not to drag pans on to it from the hotplates, as this might scratch it, and I always wipe up any spills immediately with a damp soapy cloth. This is especially important with anything containing an acid, such as fruit juice or a simmering home-made jam or chutney.

Ovens

Because the heat of most of the ovens is so high and constant, there is never any risk of spilled foods spoiling or causing smells or germs. Everything gets burned away, and any carbonised deposits can simply be brushed out of the ovens. The wire brush provided with the Aga can be used to scrub away any spills that have been burnt on. Do so very quickly, brushing top, sides and base. On a more frequent basis, I use an old dust-pan and brush. Again you must work very quickly.

To prevent the build-up of grease on the doors of your ovens, put any pans containing foods which might splatter – grilled, fried, sautéed, even stir-fried – to the back of the oven, as far from the doors as possible.

To clean inside the oven doors, wipe them frequently. To spring-clean them, wear oven gloves to lift them carefully off their hinges. Only do one door at a time to minimise heat loss – and not just before you want to do a lot of high-temperature cooking! Place the door on a towel on a strong working surface, enamel side down, and leave to cool a little. Use a Brillo pad to get rid of any greasy deposits, then wipe clean with a warm soapy cloth. Wipe the enamel front of the doors with a warm soapy cloth, rinse and wipe with a damp cloth. When dry, polish the outside of the doors with a wax spray polish and replace the doors.

Never immerse the doors in water as they contain insulating material.

Warming Plate

The four-oven cooker's Warming Plate is made from aluminium (in older models) and hard anodised aluminium (newer models). The older one could be removed by corner screws and lifted off to be cleaned; newer plates are permanently fixed. Clean both by simply using Astonish, or a damp soapy cloth.

Boiling and Simmering Plates

These are made of cast iron. Allow spills to simply burn off, then remove any residue with the wire brush supplied. It is particularly important to keep the plates free of burnt-on particles as these could prevent good contact between the base of saucepans and the hotplate. To clean under and around the outside trim rings, you can lift them out – but be careful, using oven gloves and a heavy fork or skewer. Use a wire brush to clean and vacuum out any crumbs before replacing the rings.

Always brush the plates with the wire brush after making toast, as even a few errant crumbs can cause a kettle to take up to *one minute* longer to boil!

The Shiny Hotplate Lids

These are shiny on top, and the insulating liners are made of aluminium. To keep the tops clean and shiny, wipe over with a damp soapy cloth, followed by a wet cloth, then polish with a clean dry cloth. To keep the shine, cover with a towel or cloth before putting pans or roasting trays directly on them. This could scratch the surface.

To clean the inner lid liners, first of all open one lid up to allow it to cool a little. You could also lessen the heat coming up from the plate by covering the plate with the plain shelf. Wipe the aluminium with a thick, damp soapy cloth, then use a wet Brillo pad held firmly with a large damp cloth. Wipe over and dry.

Servicing

To help your Aga run efficiently, you should have it serviced regularly. The instructions that came with your Aga should tell you of the frequency required. Your Aga Authorised Distributor or Aga Shop will be able to advise.

When switching on after servicing, you may need to adjust the temperature control. Simply make a note of the position of the mercury on the heat indicator for two or three mornings, and adjust as described in the operating instructions until the mercury remains at the centre line.

THE AGA WAY OF COOKING

The Aga way of cooking is not *radically* different, but it undeniably *is* different. It's a case of re-educating yourself in a very logical way. After a short while it will all be second nature.

As the Aga works on the principle of storing heat within the cooker, the aim is to cook mostly in the ovens so that as much heat as possible is retained. If you cooked too much on the top, the plate *and* oven temperatures would drop. This means rethinking the way you go about many things usually done on the top of a stove or under a grill. It is also very daunting to suddenly have to operate without specific oven cooking temperatures, especially if you've been cooking conventionally for years. With the Aga it's a case of changing a food's *position* in the oven, or by choosing a *different* oven.

It would probably be useful to go through the qualities of the individual ovens, making suggestions as you go.

▰▏▰▰ *The Roasting Oven*

The Roasting Oven on both two-oven and four-oven Agas is very hot, much hotter than a conventional oven. You have top and bottom heat, heat from the sides, heat from the back and reflected heat from the door, so it is a truly all-round heat. It is hottest at the top, nearly as hot at the very bottom, and slightly cooler in the middle. I've found the back of the oven is often hotter than the front, and in older Agas, the

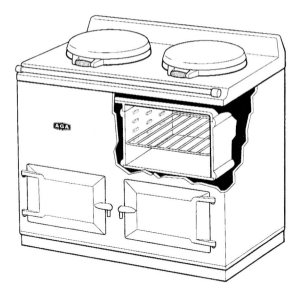

The runners for shelves in any of the Aga ovens are numbered from the top.

back left. The oven – and the cooker in general – is hottest first thing in the morning, because it has had a build-up of heat overnight. Its usual temperature is the equivalent of about 240°C/480°F/Gas mark 9.

The Roasting Oven has four sets of runners in the sides. They number from top to the bottom. Use these to vary the heat you need. The handles of any cooking dishes need to be heatproof for the Roasting Oven.

Roasting

Obviously the oven is good for roasting, but different things need to go in at different levels. The top is best for browning and crisping, the middle for roasts of meat and fish, and the bottom for roast potatoes and other roast vegetables. With some roasts – leg of lamb or duck, say – you may need to start in the Roasting Oven, then finish off in the Simmering Oven (for details refer to my original Aga book, page 28).

Baking

Two-oven Aga owners, who lack a Baking Oven, have to use the plain shelf and the runners to moderate the heat of the Roasting Oven when they want to bake.

Pastries and bread are wonderful in the Roasting Oven. Cook puff pastry pies towards the top, bread and quiches on or near the floor (bread tins on a gridshelf). The heat from the floor of the oven is for me the greatest asset of the Aga, an intense heat coming up into pans placed directly on the floor. For one thing, you will never have to blind-bake pastry again (except something like lemon meringue pie which has a very short cooking time). Put the quiche or tart tin on the floor of the oven and get a crispy, browned pastry bottom as well as sides. Bake lasagnes and similar made-up dishes towards the foot of the oven; brown them at the top of the oven before serving.

Because the oven is so consistently hot, and you cannot turn any controls down, you may have to start something like a less tender roast or a custard-based pudding, a fruit crumble or pastry pie in the Roasting Oven until the perfect colour or set, then move them to the Simmering Oven to continue cooking.

Frying and Grilling

You can shallow-fry on the floor of the Roasting Oven, in a suitable frying pan in a little hot fat. You can also grill bacon, etc., at the top of the oven on the grill rack in the roasting tin. Grill chops and steaks on a preheated ridged grill pan on the floor of the Roasting Oven. Brown the tops of shepherd's pie, cheese-topped dishes or crumbles at the top of the oven.

Instead of conventional frying or grilling, use the ovens to their best advantage. Brown-grill a chicken breast at the top of the oven, but to brown its underneath, put the dish on the floor of the oven. To cook and brown fish cakes put some Lift-Off or a greased baking sheet on the floor of the oven, turning them once – easier and much healthier than frying.

⬛⬛ *The Baking Oven in the Four-oven Aga*

Only four-oven Agas have a Baking Oven. Like the Roasting Oven, it has all-round heat, and is hotter at the top than the base. Its usual temperature is the equivalent of about 190°C/380°F/Gas mark 5.

The Baking Oven has four sets of runners. Use these to vary the amount of heat you need, as well as the plain shelf as appropriate. The handles of any cooking dishes need to be heatproof in the Baking Oven.

Anything that requires a moderate temperature can be cooked in the Baking Oven. It is ideal for many small cakes, biscuits and breads. Bake small cakes, fatless sponges and lasagne towards the top, biscuits, brownies, muffins, breads, baked fish and crumbles towards the middle, and sweet rolls, Victoria sponges and cheesecakes towards the base (usually on the grid shelf on the floor).

Many foods can be cooked in the Baking Oven instead of in the Roasting Oven, but they will obviously take longer. Some dishes started in the Roasting Oven can be completed in the Baking Oven.

⬛|⬛⬛ *The Simmering Oven*

On the two-oven Aga, the Simmering Oven is bottom right; on the four-oven Aga, it is top left. The heat, as ever, is all-round, but it is fairly gentle, with the top of the oven the hottest part. The usual temperature is the equivalent of 110–120°C/ 220–250°F/Gas mark ¼–½, and more modern Agas will be slightly hotter. It has one set of runners in the middle in the four-oven Aga and three sets of runners in the two-oven Aga.

Most foods put into the Simmering Oven will have begun their cooking elsewhere – on the hotplates or in one of the other ovens. (Rich fruit cakes and meringues are two exceptions to this rule.) It is very useful to have an oven in which you know things won't come to much harm. If you have a two-oven Aga, this is where you will keep things hot. But do remember that it does actually *cook*, so if you have to keep things warm, *under*cook them to begin with. Put them on a cold plate, and cover them with foil or clingfilm (you can use the latter in the Simmering Oven – very useful to be able to see through the clear film). I actually do a lot of reheating in my Simmering Oven. I've suggested in the recipes that you do this in the Roasting Oven, because most people haven't thought ahead, and are in a hurry. In the slower oven, of course, it will take about three times longer.

Principally the Simmering Oven is used for the slow cooking of casseroles and stews, soups and stocks. Bring things to the boil on the hotplates first, then put in the Simmering Oven. There's no better way to cook root vegetables (see opposite) or rice, or indeed to defrost some frozen foods. I also like very much to dry tomatoes, and the Simmering Oven is perfect for this (see page 147). I make my marmalade in this oven, pushing a plate on top of the whole oranges so that they remain below the level of the water. One of the major benefits of this is that the house doesn't smell of marmalade, see my original Aga book.

If you have an old Aga, the Simmering Oven may be slower: what you might have to do is bring whatever you have cooking to the boil every half hour or so on the hotplate, then return it to the oven to go on cooking. A Christmas cake, a small joint of gammon or an oxtail could cook overnight in an older Simmering Oven.

■■ *The Warming Oven in the Four-oven Aga*

Only four-oven Agas have a Plate-warming Oven. As the name suggests, it has a very low heat, perfect for warming plates and dishes. Although cooler than the Simmering Oven, it can be used in similar ways. It has one set of runners.

I keep a pile of plates warm in my oven for everyday eating; that way I never forget! You can also make stocks and porridge in this oven, dry fruit and vegetables, as well as rest joints before carving, keep sauces warm, and keep covered meals warm for any late arrivals.

The Boiling and Simmering Plates

Use the Boiling Plate when an intense heat is required – when boiling green vegetables, stir-frying, grilling meat in a ridged grill pan, starting off a vegetable dish destined for one of the ovens, and for boiling water and making toast. Many things started on the Boiling Plate can be moved to the Simmering Plate to continue cooking more slowly. Use the gentler heat of the Simmering Plate for boiling milk, for making sauces, and as a griddle for drop scones (Scotch pancakes). Clean it thoroughly first, and grease it lightly. If I am in a great hurry, and too lazy to use the Aga toaster, I sometimes toast bread straight on the Simmering Plate, without using the toaster, turning it once.

Because the circular hotplates are so large, several pans could be used on them at one time. In general, though, choose large pans that will cover as much of the plate surface as possible, in order to maximise cooking heat and reduce heat loss. *Always* close the hotplate lids when not using the plates.

AGA TECHNIQUES

As I've said, it's all about slightly changing the way you think about cooking. It won't take you long to grasp, and then you'll wonder why you didn't change to an Aga years before! The main principle of Aga cooking is using the ovens instead of the top, and although this could mean a slightly longer cooking time, you will save on heat. Another major Aga technique involves organisation and planning in advance. This will already be part of every cook's thinking, but it can really help with the Aga, especially if you are entertaining. When you know you will be busy and the ovens will be full, you need to be well prepared. Yorkshire puddings, roast potatoes and lots of elements of a Sunday lunch, say, can be cooked or part-cooked the day before, and then briefly reheated when you need them. Saying this, isn't it wonderful to have the Aga constantly hot, tempting one to cook!

Make Full Use of the Ovens

Fried Onions or Leeks

Instead of just frying on the fast Boiling Plate and watching for, say, 10 minutes, start them off in butter or oil on the Boiling Plate, then cover with the lid of the pan and put them in the Simmering Oven to become tender, about 20–30 minutes. You are not losing heat, you don't have to watch them, and you have saved time. You simply have to bring them back on to the Boiling Plate to boil off excess water and in the case of onions, let them brown.

Root Vegetables

Potatoes, carrots, parsnips, celeriac, etc., can be very successfully cooked in the oven, and once you have got used to it, you'll find there is no better way. Prepare your root vegetable as usual, bring to the boil in salted water on top of the Aga, and boil for about 5 minutes. Drain off all the water, put the lid back on the pan, then put the pan on the floor of the Simmering Oven. The vegetable will go on cooking in its own steam, which is very healthy, and will not stick to the pan because of the gentle heat. Again it will take longer, but it's worth it. New potatoes will take about 30 minutes, old about 40; celeriac about 30 minutes, baby carrots only about 5–10 minutes. The time will vary according to the size that the vegetables have been cut into.

Browning Meat for a Casserole

This can be done in the Roasting Oven. Grease the bottom of the large roasting pan, and put the pieces of meat in. Place the pan at the top of the Roasting Oven and leave the meat to become brown. When it is, drain off any juices (save them to add to the stew), then put the pan on the floor of the Roasting Oven for the under parts of the meat to brown. This will take about 45 minutes, but you don't have to stand over a couple of pans on top of the cooker, and there's no splattering, steam or smell.

Rice

Cook rice by the absorption method in the Simmering Oven instead of on top. Wash rice, add water and salt (225g/8 oz basmati or easy-cook long-grain to 350ml/ 12 fl oz water; the same weight of brown rice to 420ml/ 14 fl oz water), and bring to the boil on the Boiling Plate. Stir, replace the lid, and put on the floor of the oven for 15–20 minutes (basmati, easy-cook long-grain) or 40–45 minutes (brown).

Peas, Beans and Lentils

Cook pulses in the Simmering Oven as well. Wash, soak overnight and cover with fresh water. Bring to the boil on the Boiling Plate, boil for 10 minutes, then transfer to the oven. Cook until tender, about 1–3 hours depending on type.

Stock

Most people think of a stockpot simmering away gently on top of the stove, and don't realise stock can be very successfully made in the oven of an Aga. Simply gather together all your ingredients, brown the bones if needed in the Roasting Oven (beef or veal for about 45 minutes), then put into a pan (I use my preserving pan for chicken and veal stocks) with enough water to cover. Bring to the boil on the Boiling Plate, then transfer to the floor of the Simmering Oven. Leave overnight for beef, veal, game, etc., 8–9 hours for raw chicken bones, 1 hour for fish, 3–4 hours for a family stock (made with leftover joint or chicken bones), 3 hours for a vegetable stock. Stocks can be simmered even more slowly in the Warming Oven overnight.

Steamed Puddings

Steam your Christmas pudding. First bring to the boil on the Boiling Plate then cover and transfer to the Simmering Plate for about 30 minutes. Transfer the covered pan to the Simmering Oven for about 12 hours. There is no steam in your kitchen, and the water rarely, if ever, boils away. The cake baker is an ideal pan to use; cook totally in the Roasting Oven, topping up with water as necessary.

Plan Ahead

Perfect Roast Potatoes or Parsnips

If serving roast potatoes and roast parsnips, prepare and pre-roast them the day before in the Roasting Oven until just beginning to colour. (You will need much less fat when cooking in the Aga than in a conventional oven.) Cut the tips off the parsnips first, as they always brown far too quickly (use them in another dish). Discard all the fat from the pan, leave the vegetables in the pan, cover with foil and put them in the fridge. The next day, you can give them a blast in the Roasting Oven to brown them and finish the cooking. Parsnips take less time than potatoes (see *English Roast Vegetables*, page 140).

Gravy

If you're doing a roast you can make the gravy the day before with stock, ready to mix with the juices from the meat and brought to the boil at the last minute.

Yorkshire Puddings

Many people have problems cooking Yorkshire puddings in the Aga after the beef is done because the temperature in the Roasting Oven has dropped. Here's the answer. Cook the Yorkshire puddings first thing in the morning when the Aga is hottest. Leave them in their tins when cooked and put them in the larder. Reheat them in the centre of the Roasting Oven for about 8 minutes, when they will be ready to serve. (My new recipe for the best Yorkshires is: 100g/4 oz plain flour, 2 whole eggs, 1 extra egg yolk, and 225ml/ 8 fl oz milk. Double for the large roasting tin.)

Heating Serving Dishes

If you have no room for awkwardly shaped things like a gravy boat or soup tureen in the Plate-warming Oven (or Simmering Oven on the two-oven Aga), put them at the back of the Aga well in advance of your meal. They will absorb more than enough heat throughout the day.

Making the Most of the Top Heat of the Aga

Melt bowls of chocolate or butter simply by leaving at the back of the Aga. Jams and honey will be easier to spread if warmed on the Aga or in a gentle oven. The flour for bread can be gently warmed on the Warming Plate of the Aga, or the work surface next to the Aga; a bread dough left to rise will love that warmth as well. I usually slide a tea-towel underneath the bowl. Yoghurt can be made at the back of the Aga too instead of using a yoghurt maker (see *The Aga Book* for details, page 139).

Overnight Porridge

My recipe for porridge is: 75g (3 oz) pinhead (medium) oatmeal, and a generous 600ml (20 fl oz) water. Bring the water to the boil in a saucepan on the Boiling Plate. Transfer to the Simmering Plate, add the oatmeal and stir well. Simmer for about 3 minutes. Cover and transfer to the grid shelf on the floor of the Simmering Oven and leave overnight. To serve, stir well and serve with salt, dried fruit, brown sugar or golden syrup.

If using the normal quick rolled oats, add to measured cold liquid, cover and leave at the back of the Aga overnight: next morning your porridge is ready.

Oven Space

Plan your oven space in advance when entertaining. Put a roast at the back of the Roasting Oven, where it's slightly hotter, potatoes at the front. Put vegetables or other foods in dishes that will fit side by side in one of the ovens. Learn to stack pans in the ovens, inverting lids if necessary, so that one pan can stand on another. Put the foods you want to serve first closest to the oven door.

Other Aga Benefits

Warming and Drying

An Aga quickly becomes the centre of the house, and keeps the kitchen permanently warm. That warmth is ideal for drying in a number of ways. As you walk from the damp outside into a kitchen with an Aga, it's almost automatic to hang your scarf on the rail, put your anorak on the Simmering Plate cover, and lean your bottom up against the Aga to have a general warm-up!

Damp Pet Food

If you have grain or bird or dog food that is slightly damp, put it at the back of the Aga to get dry again.

Wet Shoes

Anything that needs airing – shoes, boots, etc. – can be packed with newspaper and put on the floor next to the Aga. Trainers can now be washed in the washing machine, and they can be dried next to the Aga or even in the Warming Oven if you have a four-oven Aga.

Airing

Clothes and fabrics can be folded and hung on the Aga rail, or on a shelf or rail above the Aga, and then they can go straight into the drawer or wardrobe afterwards.

Family Ironing

Clothes that do not need to be perfectly ironed can be 'ironed' on the Aga. Smooth them over by hand, and arrange on top of the Simmering Plate lid, making sure they do not drape over the handles of the insulating lids. Turn once, and they should be near perfect! Sheets, pillowcases and duvet covers made from 50 per cent cotton/50 per cent polyester need little ironing if carefully folded, slightly damp, on the Simmering Plate lid or on the rail. Be careful not to let anything drape over the vents of the burner door. Don't put anything on the Boiling Plate lid, as it will scorch.

Kitchen Utensils

Use the heat of the Aga to dry roasting tins and pans or awkward kitchen implements such as graters, the food processor blade, etc. Put on a tea-towel at the back of the Aga.

Drying Herbs and Flowers

Hang bunches of herbs or flowers from a rail or shelf above the Aga to dry slowly in the rising warmth. The herbs I dry most are bay leaves and rosemary. Selected vegetables and fruits can be dried as well: hang strings of chillies or apple rings above the Aga.

ENJOY YOUR AGA!

NOTES ON RECIPES

1   All the eggs used are large.

2   **V** This symbol indicates recipes that are suitable for vegetarians, but please note that some of them include dairy products.

3   ⦂ This symbol represents a two-oven Aga.

     ⦂⦂ This symbol represents a four-oven Aga.

4   The runners for shelves in the Roasting, Baking and Simmering Ovens are numbered from the top. The 'second set of runners' is therefore second down from the top.

5   Each recipe has instructions on how to prepare ahead, to freeze, to thaw, to reheat and to cook in a conventional oven.

FIRST COURSES

I can't think of anything more satisfying than a good soup with which to start a meal. Indeed it can often be served as a lunch by itself, accompanied by some warmed crusty bread. I've included a couple of soup recipes here; use your own stock if you have some to hand, if not a cube will do. The advantage of making stock at home is that it can happily simmer away in the Aga for hours without steaming up the kitchen or sending its aroma throughout the house. The low heat of the Simmering Oven (even the Plate-warming Oven if you have a four-oven Aga) is perfect for home-made stocks. Stocks and soups freeze well.

Pâtés, terrines and soufflés are wonderful cooked in the Aga. Serve with a green leaf salad and fresh bread. These would also be delicious as a light lunch or evening first course. I've given a few suggestions for eats to go with drinks as well, because often a few delicious morsels given to your guests before dinner can actually replace a formal first course.

Very few recipes are last-minute, and most of them are capable of being made ahead and reheated or served cold. I think most people want to get things ready in advance so they have no last-minute panics!

WATERCRESS AND CELERIAC SOUP

Celeriac is a late summer and winter vegetable. You have to peel it fairly thickly as it is such a knobbly shape. You might need to pop it in a little acidulated water (water with lemon juice) to prevent it discolouring after peeling.

Serves 6

2 bunches of watercress
65g (2½ oz) butter
1 large onion, sliced
350g (12 oz) celeriac, peeled weight, cubed

40g (1½ oz) plain flour
1.2 litres (40 fl oz) chicken stock
salt and freshly ground black pepper
about 300ml (10 fl oz) milk, boiling
a little single cream

1 Wash the watercress but do not remove the stalks. Trim off a small bunch of leaves to use for garnish if not freezing.

2 Melt the butter in a saucepan on the Boiling Plate and gently toss the onion and celeriac, not letting them brown. Add the flour, mix well, then add the stock and seasoning. Bring to the boil, then simmer, covered, for 5 minutes on the Simmering Plate. Transfer to the floor of the Simmering Oven, covered, for 30 minutes until tender.

3 Add the watercress, with stalks, and simmer for a further 5 minutes on the Simmering Plate. Purée the soup in a processor or liquidiser, return the soup to the pan and add the boiling milk to make the required consistency. Check seasoning.

4 To serve, stir in a little cream and sprinkle each serving with the reserved finely chopped watercress leaves. Do not keep the soup hot for any length of time, as it will go grey in colour.

TO PREPARE AHEAD   The soup can be completed to the end of stage 3, quickly cooled, then stored in a sealed container in the fridge for up to 2 days.

TO FREEZE   Pour the soup into a freezer container, cool, cover and freeze for up to 1 month.

TO THAW   Thaw for about 8 hours in the container at room temperature, or overnight in the fridge.

TO REHEAT   Reheat in a pan on the Boiling or Simmering Plate to just below boiling point, stirring until well blended.

TO COOK IN A CONVENTIONAL OVEN   Cook the soup on top of the hob in the usual way.

LEEK AND STILTON SOUP

This is a winter soup essentially. You will see that I suggest coarsely grating the Stilton cheese. I find crumbling it totally unsatisfactory, as it is sticky and gets under the nails! It is worth infusing the milk, if you have time, with the bay and nutmeg.

Serves 6–8

350g (12 oz) leeks	1.2 litres (40 fl oz) chicken stock
600ml (20 fl oz) milk	salt and freshly ground black pepper
2 bay leaves	150g (5 oz) Stilton cheese, coarsely
a little freshly grated nutmeg	grated
75g (3 oz) butter	a little single cream
75g (3 oz) plain flour	fresh parsley or chives, chopped

1 Cut the leeks into four lengthways and shred finely. Wash and drain thoroughly.

2 Measure the milk into a small saucepan, heat until hand hot on the Simmering Plate, then add the bay leaves and a grating of nutmeg. Cover the pan and leave to infuse on the floor of the Simmering Oven for 20 minutes or so.

3 Melt the butter in a pan on the Boiling Plate, add the flour and cook for a few moments. Add the strained hot milk, stirring well, then add the stock. Stir in the leeks, season (using very little salt because of the salty cheese), and bring to the boil. Transfer to the Simmering Plate and simmer for a few minutes. Add the cheese and stir well. Cover and transfer to the floor of the Simmering Oven for 15 minutes: the cheese should be melted and the leeks tender.

4 Check the seasoning. If a little too thick, thin down with milk or stock. Serve with a little added single cream, and garnish with freshly chopped parsley or chives.

TO PREPARE AHEAD   The soup can be made, quickly cooled and stored in the fridge for up to 2 days.

TO FREEZE   Cool, pack and freeze the soup at the end of stage 3 for up to 1 month.

TO THAW   Thaw the soup at room temperature for 8 hours or overnight in the fridge.

TO REHEAT   Reheat the soup on the Simmering Plate. Complete stage 4.

TO COOK IN A CONVENTIONAL OVEN   Cook on the hob in the usual way.

FRESH VEGETABLE TERRINE V

This light and very low-calorie terrine is best eaten within 2 days. Take care to season it well, and you can serve with your favourite French dressing, made with lemon juice instead of vinegar if liked.

Serves 6

vegetable oil

350g (12 oz) carrots, peeled weight,
    roughly cut

a walnut-sized piece of fresh root ginger,
    peeled and cut into small pieces

salt and freshly ground black pepper

350g (12 oz) celeriac, peeled weight,
    roughly cut

350g (12 oz) broccoli

3 eggs (1 for each purée)

fresh dill or parsley for decoration

1 Well grease and base line with non-stick baking paper a 900g (2 lb) loaf tin.

2 Cook the carrot and ginger together in boiling salted water for 5 minutes on the Boiling Plate. Drain off all water and transfer to the floor of the Simmering Oven for a further 15 minutes until just done. Cook the celeriac in a similar way.

3 Cut the stalks off the broccoli and cook in boiling salted water until al dente, then add the 'florets' and cook for a further minute. Drain and refresh with cold water.

4 Starting with the carrot and ginger, followed by the celeriac and then the broccoli, process each vegetable separately, adding one of the eggs to each, and seasoning. Blend until just smooth and carefully spoon first the carrot mixture, then the celeriac, then the broccoli in layers into the loaf tin. Cover the tin tightly with greased foil. Stand the loaf tin in the small roasting tin and pour in enough boiling water to come half way up the sides of the loaf tin.

5 ⦂ Bake in the Roasting Oven on the grid shelf on the floor, with the cold plain shelf above on the second set of runners, for an hour or until set.

⦂⦂ Bake in the Baking Oven on the grid shelf on the floor for an hour until set.

6 Allow to cool in the tin. Slide a knife round the edge of the tin, and turn out on to a plate. Serve sliced with a lemony French dressing, and decorate with dill or parsley.

TO PREPARE AHEAD Cook and purée the vegetables ahead. Layer in the tin as in stage 4, cover and put in the fridge for up to 6 hours until ready to cook.

TO FREEZE Not suitable.

TO COOK IN A CONVENTIONAL OVEN Cook in the oven preheated to 180°C/350°F/ Gas mark 4 for 1 hour or until firm.

WILD MUSHROOMS ON FIELD MUSHROOMS V

This makes a delicious starter, but is particularly good served as a supper dish for vegetarians. For this recipe, take advantage of some of the wonderful mixtures of mushrooms that some supermarkets are selling in a single pack. Or use 450g (1 lb) chestnut mushrooms alone.

Serves 6

6 large flat mushrooms, about 10cm (4 in) in diameter	300ml (10 fl oz) pouring double cream
about 3 tablespoons olive oil	juice of ½ lemon
salt and freshly ground black pepper	175g (6 oz) shiitake mushrooms, sliced
25g (1 oz) butter	175g (6 oz) oyster mushrooms, sliced
2 shallots, finely chopped	175g (6 oz) chestnut mushrooms, sliced
2 cloves garlic, finely chopped	1 tablespoon chopped fresh parsley

1 Twist the central stalks from the flat mushrooms and reserve. Wipe the caps with kitchen paper while heating the olive oil in a frying pan on the Boiling Plate. Fry the mushrooms, gill side down, for 5 minutes, turning them over half way through the cooking time. Place them in a baking dish just large enough to hold the mushrooms snugly in one layer, season and keep warm.

2 Add the butter to the pan, stir in the shallot and garlic and cook for a few minutes on the Boiling Plate. Cover and transfer to the Simmering Oven for about 10 minutes to soften. Put on the Boiling Plate for a minute to drive off any liquid before adding the cream. Boil to reduce to a thick sauce, then add the lemon juice and sliced mushrooms, along with the sliced flat mushroom stalks. Season well, and toss the mushrooms in the sauce over the heat for a few minutes. Check seasoning.

3 Top each flat mushroom with the mushroom sauce, sprinkle with parsley and serve at once, with a few salad leaves.

TO PREPARE AHEAD Complete stage 1, cooling the mushrooms quickly, then cover and chill. Complete stage 2, cool, cover and chill. Keep for up to 24 hours.

TO FREEZE Not suitable.

TO REHEAT Spoon the cold mushroom sauce on to the large mushrooms and reheat in the Roasting Oven for about 10 minutes, until piping hot.

TO COOK IN A CONVENTIONAL OVEN Cook on the hob in the normal way. Keep the large mushrooms warm in a moderate oven, 180°C/350°F/Gas mark 4.

MUSHROOM AND HERB CREAMS **V**

A slightly different and light first course, which is also perfect for a summer lunch when it will serve four. This recipe is a bonus if some of your guests are vegetarian.

Serves 8

15g (½ oz) butter	DRESSING
350g (12 oz) chestnut mushrooms, finely sliced (use buttons if chestnuts aren't available)	1 generous teaspoon coarse grain mustard
1 egg	3 teaspoons caster sugar
3 egg yolks	juice of 1 lemon
300ml (10 fl oz) double cream	4 tablespoons olive oil
65ml (2½ fl oz) milk	
3 tablespoons chopped fresh parsley	SALAD
1 tablespoon chopped fresh marjoram	about 100g (4 oz) salad leaves (rocket, lamb's lettuce, curly endive, radicchio, land cress, lettuce)
a little freshly grated nutmeg	
salt and freshly ground black pepper	

1 Melt the butter in a medium pan on the Boiling Plate, add the mushrooms, and stir over the heat for a minute or two. Cover and transfer to the floor of the Simmering Oven for 10 minutes.

2 Grease eight ramekin dishes 7.5cm (3 in) in diameter or 75ml (3 fl oz) in capacity very thoroughly, and stand in the small roasting tin. Put the eggs, cream, milk, herbs, nutmeg and seasoning into a measuring jug and whisk thoroughly.

3 Remove the mushrooms from the Simmering Oven, uncover and boil off any liquid on the Boiling Plate. Divide evenly between the dishes standing in the small roasting tin, and pour the egg mixture over the mushrooms.

4 Pour boiling water round the ramekin dishes until half way up the side of the roasting tin. Cook in the Roasting Oven, with the grid shelf on the lowest set of runners, for about 15–20 minutes or until firm and just beginning to brown on top. Check after 10 minutes, and turn round if necessary.

5 Remove from the oven and leave to become cold in the roasting tin of water. Run a knife round the side of each one, tap the sides and turn out with the tops uppermost.

6 Make the dressing by measuring all the dressing ingredients into a clean jam jar and giving it a good shake. Season to taste. Arrange the salad on eight plates and dress lightly just before serving.

7 To reheat, slide the mushroom creams on to a baking sheet lined with Lift-Off paper or non-stick baking parchment. Cook in the same position in the Roasting Oven as before for about 10–15 minutes or until hot and sizzling. Using a fish slice, place each one on top of a pile of salad and serve immediately.

TO PREPARE AHEAD   The herb creams can be made a day ahead. Allow to cool completely and keep in the fridge.

TO FREEZE   Not suitable.

TO COOK IN A CONVENTIONAL OVEN   Cook at 180°C/350°F/Gas mark 4, in a bain-marie for about 20 minutes until firm.

PROTECTING ALUMINIUM

If you are using an aluminium roasting tin as a bain-marie, put a wedge of lemon in the cooking water to prevent a black line appearing in the tin.

CARLTON PÂTÉ

Chicken livers are very reasonable to buy. This pâté makes a good first course. Any left over may be used as a sandwich filling.

Serves 8

1 × 225g (8 oz) tub of chicken livers	175g (6 oz) full-fat cream cheese
225g (8 oz) butter, softened	2 teaspoons lemon juice
1 small onion, finely chopped	1 scant tablespoon soy sauce
350g (12 oz) button mushrooms, sliced	1 tablespoon chopped fresh parsley
50g (2 oz) fresh breadcrumbs	salt and freshly ground black pepper
lots of freshly grated nutmeg	

1 Trim the chicken livers. Melt 75g (3 oz) of the butter in a large non-stick frying pan on the Boiling Plate and sauté the chicken livers until lightly cooked. Lift out of the pan and set aside. Add the onion to the pan, stir, then cover and transfer the pan to the floor of the Simmering Oven to soften for about 10 minutes.

2 Return the pan to the Boiling Plate, add the mushrooms and fry briskly for a few minutes. Stir in the breadcrumbs and then allow to cool.

3 Purée the mushroom mixture with the chicken livers in the processor. Add the remaining 150g (5 oz) butter, the nutmeg, cheese, lemon juice, soy sauce and parsley, and purée again until evenly blended. Season well, and taste.

4 Turn into a pâté dish or small terrine and chill in the fridge before serving, with hot brown toast and butter or good French bread and a few leaves.

TO PREPARE AHEAD This pâté will keep, covered in the fridge, for up to 3 days.

TO FREEZE Cover and freeze the pâté for up to 3 months.

TO THAW Thaw at room temperature for a few hours.

TO COOK IN A CONVENTIONAL OVEN Cook on the hob in the usual way.

WARM COURGETTE AND GOAT'S CHEESE MOUSSELINES V

These are unusual and light individual mousselines made in ramekin dishes, then turned out and served warm on a bed of tomato and basil salad.

Serves 6

vegetable oil	2 tablespoons chopped fresh basil
1 small onion, finely chopped	salt and freshly ground black pepper
350g (12 oz) small courgettes, finely chopped	freshly grated nutmeg
1 × 175g (6 oz) tub of soft goat's cheese	TOMATO AND BASIL SALAD
2 eggs	12 medium tomatoes, skinned and sliced
40g (1½ oz) fresh white breadcrumbs	2 tablespoons chopped fresh basil
25g (1 oz) Parmesan, freshly grated	3 tablespoons salad dressing

1 Lightly oil six medium ramekins, and line bases with non-stick baking parchment.

2 Heat 2 tablespoons of the oil in a pan on the Boiling Plate, and sauté the onion for a few minutes. Cover and transfer to the floor of the Simmering Oven for 5–10 minutes. Return to the hotplate and quickly stir-fry the courgettes for 2 minutes. Allow to cool slightly.

3 Place the goat's cheese and eggs in the processor and blend together until smooth. Add all the remaining ingredients (including the cooled courgette and onion), season lightly and blend to a coarse purée.

4 Spoon the mixture into the six prepared ramekins.

5 ⁝ Put the ramekins in the small roasting tin half filled with boiling water, on the grid shelf on the floor of the Roasting Oven, with the cold plain shelf on the second set of runners above. Bake for about 20 minutes until set.

⁞⁞ Bake in the roasting tin half filled with boiling water on the grid shelf on the floor of the Baking Oven for about 20 minutes until set.

6 Allow to rest for a further 5 minutes. Carefully turn out on to individual plates with the dressed tomato and basil salad then peel off the disc of paper. Serve at once.

TO PREPARE AHEAD   Prepare to the end of stage 4, cover and keep in the fridge for up to 8 hours.

TO FREEZE   Not suitable.

TO COOK IN A CONVENTIONAL OVEN   Cook at 180°C/350°F/Gas mark 4 in a bain-marie for about 20 minutes until set.

HOT SPICED AUBERGINE STACKS V

A fresh veggie first course. The aubergine is not buttered or fried, therefore cutting down on the fat and an extra process. Choose the goat's cheese that comes in a barrel shape – you need six slices. Metal cooking rings can be bought mail order from Lakeland Limited (phone the Windermere headquarters, 015394 88100, for information) or from good cookshops. You could make these stacks in individual Yorkshire pudding tins – line the bases with greased discs of baking parchment first.

Serves 6

I large aubergine, sliced into 12 × 5mm (¼ in) rings	½ teaspoon ground turmeric
a knob of butter	½–I teaspoon Tabasco sauce
I small onion, finely chopped	salt and freshly ground black pepper
I red pepper, seeded and chopped	6 slices (about 100g/4 oz) goat's cheese
3 tomatoes, skinned and chopped	paprika
½ teaspoon ground cumin	chopped fresh parsley

1 Take a baking sheet and line with Lift-Off paper or non-stick baking paper. Arrange six 7cm (2¾ in) cooking rings on the paper. Put a slice of aubergine in the base of each ring.

2 Melt the butter in a pan on the Simmering Plate, and fry the onion, pepper and tomato for a few minutes. Stir in the cumin, turmeric, Tabasco and seasoning.

3 Divide the mixture between the rings, spooning on to the aubergine slices. Top with another slice of aubergine and a slice of goat's cheese. Sprinkle with paprika.

4 Slide on to the second set of runners in the Roasting Oven and bake for about 10–15 minutes until piping hot and brown. Remove the rings, arrange on six individual plates, and garnish with chopped parsley.

TO PREPARE AHEAD   Prepare ahead, keep in the fridge for a few hours and cook fresh to serve, or cook for 10 minutes only, cool and keep in the fridge until needed, then reheat as below.

TO FREEZE   Not suitable.

TO REHEAT   Slide on to the second set of runners in the Roasting Oven and heat until piping hot, about 10 minutes.

TO COOK IN A CONVENTIONAL OVEN   Cook in the oven preheated to 220°C/425°F/ Gas mark 7 for about 15 minutes.

STILTON AND LEEK TARTS V

Make these in two Yorkshire pudding tins, each of which will make four individual tarts. It is essential to roll the pastry thinly, then line the tins with the circles of pastry to come just above the rims. Instead of making your own cheese pastry, use a 500g (18 oz) pack of bought shortcrust pastry if time is short. Serve with a salad if liked.

Makes 8

CHEESE PASTRY

175g (6 oz) plain flour
1/4 teaspoon salt
1 teaspoon English mustard powder
75g (3 oz) butter, cut into small pieces
50g (2 oz) Parmesan, grated
1 egg, beaten

FILLING

a good knob of butter
1 leek, weighing about 350g (12 oz), washed and finely sliced
100g (4 oz) Stilton cheese, coarsely grated
1 large handful of fresh parsley, coarsely chopped
2 eggs
300ml (10 fl oz) single cream
salt and freshly ground black pepper
a little freshly grated nutmeg
12 black olives, stoned and halved (optional)

1 First make the pastry. Measure the flour, salt, mustard and butter into the processor or a bowl, and process or rub in until the mixture resembles fine breadcrumbs. Add the Parmesan and beaten egg and mix again as long as it takes for the ingredients to come together. Chill for 30 minutes wrapped in clingfilm.

2 For the filling, heat the butter in a large non-stick pan on the Boiling Plate and cook the sliced leek for a few minutes. Cover, transfer to the floor of the Simmering Oven and leave for 15–20 minutes until soft. Return to the Boiling Plate to drive off any excess liquid.

3 Roll the pastry out thinly on a lightly floured work surface and, using an 11cm (4½ in) cutter, cut into eight discs. Use these to line two Yorkshire pudding trays. Chill if time allows.

4 Divide the cooled leek between the pastry-lined Yorkshire pudding tins, and top with grated cheese and chopped parsley. Beat the eggs and add the cream, nutmeg and some seasoning. Carefully pour the egg and cream mixture into the tartlets and top each one with a few halved olives if liked.

5 Bake on the grid shelf on the floor of the Roasting Oven for about 15–20 minutes. If the pastry needs a little more browning underneath, remove the grid shelf and put the tins directly on the floor for a few minutes.

TO PREPARE AHEAD   Line the Yorkshire pudding tins with pastry ahead of time. Cover and keep in the fridge. Prepare and chop the filling ingredients.

TO FREEZE   Freeze the freshly baked tarts, once cold, for up to 2 months.

TO THAW   Thaw at room temperature for 2–3 hours, or overnight in the fridge.

TO REHEAT   Put on the floor of the Roasting Oven for 10 minutes.

TO COOK IN A CONVENTIONAL OVEN   Bake the pastry blind at 200°C/400°F/ Gas mark 6 for 15 minutes, removing the paper and beans for the last 5 minutes. Reduce the oven to 180°C/350°F/Gas mark 4 and bake the filled tarts for 15–20 minutes, until the filling is set and beginning to colour.

RICOTTA ROULADES WITH TOMATO SAUCE ^V

These little filo roulades are quick and easy, but look wonderfully professional. The tomato sauce that accompanies them is a marvellous standby for all sorts of other dishes, and is good either hot or cold.

Serves 6

9 sheets filo pastry (15 × 30cm/
    6 × 12 in)
melted butter
poppy seeds

FILLING
40g (1½ oz) butter
1 red onion, finely chopped
1 × 450g (1 lb) packet of frozen leaf
    spinach, thawed and squeezed out
250g (9 oz) Ricotta cheese
100g (4 oz) Gruyère cheese, grated
¼ teaspoon freshly grated nutmeg
salt and freshly ground black pepper
2 eggs

1 For the filling, melt the butter in a small pan on the Boiling Plate, and cook the chopped onion for a minute or two. Cover and transfer to the floor of the Simmering Oven for 15 minutes, or until softened but not coloured. Combine with the rest of the filling ingredients in a bowl and set aside.

2 Lay out three separate sheets of filo, brush with melted butter and lay two more sheets on top of each, buttering between the layers – thus making three piles of three layers of filo. Cut each pile in half to make six squares.

3 Divide the cheese and spinach mixture into six and spoon across the filo squares from corner to corner. Roll up fairly tightly leaving the join on top.

4 Brush generously with melted butter and sprinkle with poppy seeds. Put the roulades on Lift-Off paper on a baking sheet in two rows of three lengthways.

5 Cook in the Roasting Oven on the grid shelf on the floor for about 15–20 minutes. Check after 5 minutes and if the ends of the pastry are beginning to brown too quickly, put the cold plain shelf on the second set of runners.

6 Serve hot with the hot Tomato Sauce (see opposite) and a mixed leaf salad.

TO PREPARE AHEAD Make the filling up to a day ahead. Cover and keep in the fridge.

TO FREEZE These freeze raw or cooked, wrapped tightly in foil, for 1 month.

TO THAW   Thaw at room temperature for about 6 hours.

TO REHEAT   Reheat on a baking sheet at the top of the Roasting Oven for about 6 minutes to crisp up.

TO COOK IN A CONVENTIONAL OVEN   Bake at 180°C/350°F/Gas mark 4 for about 15 minutes.

TOMATO SAUCE V

The first time I made this sauce it was a last-minute panic, but by softening the onion uncovered in the Roasting Oven, the whole thing was done in no time at all! Passata is bought in jars or cartons and is a thick, concentrated, smooth tomato juice.

Serves 6

15g (½ oz) butter	2 teaspoons caster sugar
1 sweet red onion, very finely chopped	salt and freshly ground black pepper
1 small clove garlic, crushed	2 sprigs fresh thyme
600ml (20 fl oz) tomato passata	

1 Melt the butter in a pan on the Boiling Plate, and cook the onion and garlic for a minute or two, stirring well. Cover and transfer to the floor of the Simmering Oven for 15 minutes.

2 Add the passata, sugar, seasoning and thyme, and boil briskly, back on the Boiling Plate, until the sugar has dissolved and the sauce is slightly thickened, about 3–4 minutes. Discard the thyme.

TO PREPARE AHEAD   Prepare, cool, cover and keep in the fridge for up to 1 week.

TO FREEZE   Freeze for up to 2 months.

TO THAW   Thaw for about 4 hours at room temperature.

TO REHEAT   Reheat on the Boiling Plate, stirring occasionally.

TO COOK IN A CONVENTIONAL OVEN   Cook on the hob in the usual way.

SWISS DOUBLE SOUFFLÉS V

Make and cook the soufflés ahead, assemble in the gratin dish without adding the cream, cover and keep in the fridge for up to 24 hours. Pour over the cream and the rest of the Parmesan just before the second stage. This also makes a delicious lunch dish, served with crusty bread and a mixed leaf salad.

Serves 6

SOUFFLÉ
100g (4 oz) leaf spinach
300ml (10 fl oz) milk
40g (1½ oz) butter
40g (1½ oz) plain flour
salt and freshly ground black pepper
¼ level teaspoon freshly grated nutmeg

50g (2 oz) Gruyère cheese, grated
3 eggs, separated
butter for greasing

TOPPING
50g (2 oz) Parmesan, grated
300ml (10 fl oz) double cream

1 Wash the spinach and shred finely. Bring to the boil in the milk on the Boiling Plate, stir well and set aside.

2 Melt the butter in a generous-sized saucepan on the Simmering Plate, remove the pan from the heat and blend in the flour. Return to the heat and cook the roux for 1 minute, stirring all the time. Add the spinach and milk a little at a time and bring to the boil, stirring constantly. Simmer until the sauce is thick and smooth. Remove the pan from the heat and beat in the salt, pepper, nutmeg and Gruyère cheese. When these are well incorporated stir in the egg yolks.

3 Whisk the egg whites until stiff and fold carefully into the sauce mixture.

4 Butter six small ramekin dishes, 9 × 4cm (3½ × 1½ in), very generously and spoon in the mixture. Place them in the small roasting tin, and pour boiling water into the tin to come half way up the dishes. Cook in the bain-marie in the Roasting Oven on the grid shelf on the floor for 15–20 minutes. After 10 minutes or when the soufflés are a perfect golden brown, turn round if necessary, and slide in the cold plain shelf on the second set of runners. Continue cooking until they are springy to the touch. Leave for 5–10 minutes in the ramekin dishes to shrink back.

5 Butter a shallow gratin dish which is large enough to hold the little soufflés without them touching each other. Sprinkle half the Parmesan on the bottom of the dish.

6 Run the blade of a small palette knife round the edges of the little soufflés, then unmould them carefully and put them into the gratin dish. Season the cream and pour over the little soufflés. Sprinkle the rest of the Parmesan over the surface, and bake in the Roasting Oven as before, but without the cold plain shelf, for another 15–20 minutes or until the soufflés have puffed up and are golden.

TO PREPARE AHEAD   Up to 48 hours ahead, turn the cooked soufflés out on to the Parmesan-dusted dish and cover with foil.

TO FREEZE   Freeze the wrapped, cooked soufflés for up to 1 month.

TO THAW   Thaw at room temperature for about 6 hours.

TO REHEAT   As from stage 5, except the soufflés are already turned out.

TO COOK IN A CONVENTIONAL OVEN   Cook in the oven preheated to 220°C/425°F/ Gas mark 7 for 15–20 minutes until golden and springy to the touch. Leave to stand for 5–10 minutes, then continue with stages 5 and 6, returning to the oven for 15–20 minutes, until golden.

CRAB CAKES

If you can get fresh crabmeat, even better. Use either white or brown meat, or a mixture of both, about 225g (8 oz). The quantities here serve six as a starter, but you can make them much smaller and have them hot with drinks.

Serves 6

25g (1 oz) butter

2 spring onions, finely chopped

25g (1 oz) plain flour

150ml (5 fl oz) milk

salt and freshly ground black pepper

2 × 170g (6 oz) tins of white crabmeat, well drained

1 tablespoon chopped fresh coriander

1 tablespoon lemon or lime juice

25g (1 oz) fresh white breadcrumbs

TO COOK

1 egg, beaten

breadcrumbs

sunflower oil for shallow-frying

1 Melt the butter in a small pan on the Simmering Plate, add the spring onions and cook gently until soft but not coloured. Add the flour, cook for 1 minute, then gradually add the milk. Season and bring to the boil, stirring – the sauce will be very thick. Allow to cool.

2 Add the drained crabmeat, coriander, lemon or lime juice and the measured breadcrumbs, and stir lightly to mix. Check seasoning.

3 Divide the mixture into twelve and make into round cake shapes. Dip the crab cakes into beaten egg and then breadcrumbs to cover. Cover and chill for about 30 minutes.

4 Heat the oil in a large non-stick frying pan on the Boiling Plate, and fry the crab cakes for about 4–5 minutes each side until golden and hot right through.

5 Drain on kitchen paper, then serve immediately with the Lime and Coriander Dressing (see opposite) and a leafy salad.

TO PREPARE AHEAD   Make the crab cakes to the end of stage 3. Cover and chill for up to 48 hours.

TO FREEZE   At the end of stage 3, pack the crab cakes in a single layer in a rigid freezerproof container and freeze for up to 1 month.

TO THAW   Thaw for about 3 hours at room temperature or overnight in the fridge.

TO COOK IN A CONVENTIONAL OVEN   Use the hob in the usual way to fry until golden brown.

LIME AND CORIANDER DRESSING V

This dressing also goes well with fish and prawns.

Serves 6

75ml (3 fl oz) sunflower oil
1 tablespoon lime juice
1 teaspoon caster sugar

1 × 1cm (½ in) piece of fresh root
  ginger, finely grated
1 tablespoon chopped fresh coriander
salt and freshly ground black pepper

1 Measure all the ingredients into a clean jam jar, shake to thoroughly mix and serve.

TO PREPARE AHEAD Make the dressing up to 2 days before it is needed, adding the coriander just before serving to keep the fresh green colour. Keep in the fridge.

TO FREEZE Not suitable.

RED HOUSE BLUES V

The name came about because I was introduced to the recipe by our dear friend Joan Heath, who lives in The Red House. This is my version of her delicious biscuits, which can be made ahead and baked as and when you need them. Remember to slightly reduce the cooking time for the smaller biscuits.

Makes about 30–40, according to size

75g (3 oz) shelled walnuts	150g (5 oz) plain flour
75g (3 oz) Stilton cheese, or any blue cheese you have left over, grated	100g (4 oz) butter, at room temperature
	salt and freshly ground black pepper
1 teaspoon English mustard powder	50g (2 oz) Parmesan, coarsely grated

1 Process the walnuts very briefly until roughly chopped, then lift out of the processor. Put the rest of the ingredients into the processor, saving one-third of the Parmesan for the topping, and process until the mixture is just beginning to form a ball. Process with the chopped walnuts for a moment.

2 Turn on to a floured surface, divide the mixture into two and roll out each part to form an even sausage shape about 15cm (6 in) long. (N.B. If you are using these as an accompaniment for cheese, make the sausage about 6cm/2½ in in diameter. If using as biscuits to have with drinks, divide the mixture again and make into even smaller rolls.) Wrap in clingfilm and chill or freeze, until the biscuit roll is really firm, so you can easily slice it into discs.

3 Slice the sausages into discs about 5mm (¼ in) thick, and spread out on a baking sheet. Sprinkle the reserved Parmesan on each biscuit.

4 **⦙** Bake on the grid shelf on the floor of the Roasting Oven with the cold plain shelf on the second set of runners, for about 10–15 minutes, watching carefully until pale golden at the edges.

⦙⦙ Bake on the grid shelf on the floor of the Baking Oven for 10–15 minutes, watching carefully. If getting too brown, slide the cold plain shelf on to the second set of runners.

5 Remove from the oven and cool on a cooling rack.

TO PREPARE AHEAD   The biscuit mixture can be made to the end of stage 2 and kept chilled for a few days or frozen (see opposite).

TO FREEZE   Freeze the uncooked mixture in rolls for up to 3 months, or pack the cooled biscuits into freezer boxes and freeze for the same time.

TO THAW   These thaw very quickly – about 1 hour in the container or, if in a huge rush, put them on the back of the Aga. When they have been frozen, it is best to crisp them up in the Simmering Oven for about 30 minutes before serving.

TO COOK IN A CONVENTIONAL OVEN   Bake in the oven preheated to 200°C/400°F/ Gas mark 6 for 15–20 minutes until a pale golden brown.

SMOKED DUCK BREAST WITH HOISIN AND MASCARPONE

The vacuum pack of smoked duck breast usually contains about 24 slices. Phileas Fogg 'Mignons Morceaux' biscuits are bought in delicatessens and supermarkets in the crisp and snack section. Cream cheese can be used instead of Mascarpone.

Makes about 24

1 × 100g (4 oz) packet of smoked, sliced duck breast	1 × 250g (9 oz) tub of Mascarpone cheese
about 24 'Mignons Morceaux' biscuits	a few tablespoons of hoisin sauce

1 Trim off any fat from the duck slices. Spread 24 little 'Mignons Morceaux' biscuits with some Mascarpone cheese. Spoon a little hoisin sauce on top.

2 Roll up a slice of smoked duck, thread a cocktail stick through it and press firmly down into the biscuit. Arrange on a dish.

TO PREPARE AHEAD   These can be made a few hours before they are needed. Cover with clingfilm and keep in the fridge.

TO FREEZE   Not suitable.

CHÈVRE AND PAPRIKA TOASTS V

Although these are good to serve with drinks, they can be offered as a first course – simply use a larger French stick. If you cannot get sun-dried tomato paste, use red pesto as an alternative.

Makes about 20–28, depending on size of loaf

1 thin French stick	about 225–275g (8–10 oz) chèvre
butter for spreading	(goat's cheese, the smaller the roll
about 2 tablespoons sun-dried	the better)
tomato paste	a little mild paprika

1 Slice the French stick into 5mm (¼ in) rounds and butter both sides. Arrange on non-stick baking parchment or Lift-Off paper on a baking sheet.

2 Spread a little of the sun-dried tomato paste on to one side of the bread. Slice the chèvre very thinly and arrange on top of the bread and tomato paste. Dust lightly with a little paprika.

3 Bake on the floor of the Roasting Oven for about 8–10 minutes, watching carefully, until melted and golden brown.

TO PREPARE AHEAD Prepare, arrange on the baking trays, cover in clingfilm and keep in the fridge for up to 3 days.

TO FREEZE Pack the uncooked made-up bread slices in a plastic freezer container, putting kitchen roll between the layers. Freeze for up to 2 months.

TO THAW There is no need to thaw them. Simply remove the bread slices from the freezer and bake immediately as in stage 3.

TO COOK IN A CONVENTIONAL OVEN Bake in the oven preheated to 220°C/425°F/ Gas mark 7, for about 8–10 minutes or until the cheese is melted and golden brown.

Clockwise from top: Chèvre and Paprika Toasts, Smoked Duck Breast with Hoisin and Mascarpone, Vegetable Samosa with Ginger and Lemon.

TAPENADE CHEESE TOASTS ^V

These are just one-bite size. If you use a fatter French loaf it will make a more substantial snack, or a quick starter.

Makes 18–24, depending on size of loaf

I long thin French loaf	about 175g (6 oz) Cheddar cheese,
olive oil for brushing	grated
I × 125g (4½ oz) jar of olive tapenade	paprika

1 Cut the loaf diagonally into 1cm (½ in) slices. Thinly brush both sides with olive oil and spread tapenade on one side. Top the tapenade side with a little grated Cheddar and a sprinkling of paprika.

2 Place on Lift-Off paper or on a well greased baking sheet, and bake on the floor or the Roasting Oven for 8–10 minutes until golden brown. Serve warm.

TO PREPARE AHEAD   Prepare, arrange on baking sheets, cover with clingfilm and keep in the fridge for up to 3 days.

TO FREEZE   Freeze the uncovered, made-up slices of bread for up to 2 months.

TO THAW   No need to thaw. Bake from frozen for about 10 minutes as in stage 2.

TO COOK IN A CONVENTIONAL OVEN   Bake in the oven preheated to 220°C/425°F/ Gas mark 7 for 8–10 minutes until melted and golden brown.

BREAD STICKING TO TOASTER?

Particularly moist or thick bread can stick to the mesh of the toaster. The answer is to heat the toaster first in the closed Boiling Plate before putting the bread in. And for thick squashy bread, don't close the hotplate lid.

MINI SAUSAGES WITH SESAME

Everyone seems to go for sausages first at a drinks party, and these are rather special, quite different from the norm.

Makes 25

450g (1 lb) mini cocktail pork sausages

2 tablespoons mango chutney, liquid only
a few sesame seeds

1 Arrange the sausages on the grill rack in the highest position in the small roasting tin. Roast on the top set of runners in the Roasting Oven until golden, about 25 minutes, turning once.

2 Whilst they are cooking, strain off the 2 tablespoons of the liquid part of the mango chutney.

3 About 5 minutes before the sausages are done, toss them in the mango chutney juice and sprinkle with sesame seeds. Return to the oven for 5 minutes until the chutney has formed a sticky glaze on the sausages.

4 Spear each sausage with a cocktail stick and serve.

TO PREPARE AHEAD Cook the sausages up to a day ahead, but do not coat. Cool completely, cover and keep in the fridge.

TO FREEZE Freeze the cooked uncoated sausages after allowing to cool completely, for up to 1 month.

TO THAW Thaw for 2–3 hours at room temperature.

TO REHEAT Toss the sausages in the mango chutney and sesame seeds as in stage 3. Reheat in the Simmering Oven for about 30 minutes.

TO COOK IN A CONVENTIONAL OVEN Cook the sausages in the oven preheated to 200°C/400°F/Gas mark 6, for about 30 minutes until nearly cooked. Toss in the mango chutney and sesame seeds and return to the oven for about 15 minutes.

TINY QUICHE LORRAINES V

This is a quick, easy way to make a party quantity of bite-size quiches, and serve them hot. Making one large quiche in a Swiss roll tin, then cutting it out into miniature rounds is far quicker and less fiddly than making individual tiny quiches. For me, the cutting-out technique wins, hands down. Also, there is only pastry on the bottom of the little quiches with this method, so it's healthier and less fattening!

Makes about 40

225g (8 oz) bought or home-made shortcrust pastry	2 tablespoons pesto
	300ml (10 fl oz) double cream
	3 eggs
FILLING	2 tablespoons chopped fresh chives
a knob of butter	75g (3 oz) Gruyère cheese, grated
1 large onion, very finely chopped	salt and freshly ground black pepper

1 Roll out the pastry thinly and use to line the base and sides of a shallow oblong Swiss roll tin about 28 × 18cm (11 x 7 in). Trim away and discard the excess pastry from the top rim of the tin, then transfer the tin to the freezer while you make the filling.

2 Heat the butter in a non-stick frying pan on the Boiling Plate. Stir in the onion, cover and transfer to the Simmering Oven for about 10 minutes until the onion is softened but not coloured. Stir in the pesto. Remove from the heat and leave to cool.

3 Combine the cream, eggs, chives and half the cheese in a bowl and beat together with a wire whisk. Season with salt and pepper.

4 Remove the pastry-lined tin from the freezer, and prick the base all over with a fork. Spread the onion mixture over the base of the pastry. Carefully pour in the quiche filling, and sprinkle with the remaining cheese.

5 Slide on to the floor of the Roasting Oven and bake for about 25–30 minutes or until puffed and golden, turning half way through. If necessary slide in the cold plain shelf on the second set of runners.

6 Leave the tin on top of a wire rack to cool. When ready, the quiche can be cut into rounds using a 3cm (1¼ in) plain cutter, or larger if you like.

7 To heat them up, arrange the 'quiches' on a baking tray and leave on the floor of the Roasting Oven for 10–15 minutes or until tinged golden and piping hot.

TO PREPARE AHEAD   Make the quiche and cut about 6 hours ahead of serving.

TO FREEZE   Cool, pack and freeze the whole quiche, still in the tin, for up to 1 month.

TO THAW   Thaw for about 4 hours at room temperature, and then cut out.

TO REHEAT   As indicated in stage 7.

TO COOK IN A CONVENTIONAL OVEN   Cook the quiche in the oven preheated to 190°C/375°F/Gas mark 5, for about 30 minutes until the filling is set and golden. Cool, then cut into rounds as above. Arrange on a baking tray and reheat in the oven at 220°C/425°F/Gas mark 7 for 10–15 minutes, until piping hot.

QUAIL'S EGGS AND CELERY V

These are a pleasant change from serving quail's eggs just with celery salt for dipping. Another good thing is that each savoury uses just a half quail's egg, which means they go twice as far!

Makes 24

1 dozen quail's eggs	celery salt
6 sticks celery	freshly ground black pepper
about 50g (2 oz) low-fat cream cheese	coarsely chopped fresh parsley

1 Hard-boil the quail's eggs for 3 minutes on the Boiling Plate, then plunge into cold water. Peel, then cut in half lengthways.

2 Remove any strings from the celery. Cut a lengthways slice from the rounded base of each stick of celery so that it sits flat on its bottom! Cut each stick into about 4cm (1½ in) slices diagonally.

3 Mix the cream cheese with celery salt and pepper to taste. Spread inside the celery boats, sprinkle with coarsely chopped parsley, and top with half an egg.

TO PREPARE AHEAD   Prepare up to a day ahead. Cover with clingfilm and keep in the fridge.

TO FREEZE   Not suitable.

PRAWN AND BOURSIN SAMOSAS

Tail ends of salmon could be used instead of the prawns. Cut into 1cm ($\frac{1}{2}$ in) pieces. If you made these samosas larger, with wider strips of filo, the samosas here, or some of the variations on the following pages, could be served as a starter.

Makes about 30

about 10 sheets filo pastry
(about 15 × 30cm/6 × 12 in)
about 50g (2 oz) butter, melted, for
brushing

FILLING
1 × 200g (7 oz) pack of frozen
cooked peeled prawns, thawed and
roughly chopped
1 × 80g (3 oz) Boursin cheese with garlic
and herbs
salt and freshly ground black pepper

1 First have all the filling ingredients to hand, the prawns (or salmon) chopped as indicated.

2 Lay the filo pastry out on a board or work surface one sheet at a time, keeping the rest covered with a damp cloth to prevent it from drying out and becoming brittle. Cut the pastry into strips about 5 × 25cm (2 × 10 in). Brush each pastry strip with melted butter.

3 Put a teaspoonful of the chopped prawns on to the bottom corner of each strip of pastry. Top with a good nut of Boursin and season with salt and black pepper.

4 Fold the pastry over so that it forms a triangle, then continue folding the triangle over itself until you reach the end of the strip. Put on to greased baking sheets or Lift-Off paper on a baking sheet.

5 Continue with more strips of filo pastry until all the prawn filling is used up. Brush the tops of each samosa with melted butter.

6 Bake on the grid shelf on the floor of the Roasting Oven for about 10 minutes, then put directly on to the floor of the Roasting Oven to brown the bases – about a further 5 minutes. Serve immediately.

TO PREPARE AHEAD   Prepare to the end of stage 5. Cover and keep in the fridge for up to a day ahead.

TO FREEZE   If fresh prawns or salmon are used, as opposed to frozen, pack and freeze the unbaked samosas for up to 1 month.

TO THAW   Thaw for about 2 hours at room temperature before baking.

TO COOK IN A CONVENTIONAL OVEN   Bake in the oven preheated to 200°C/400°F/ Gas mark 6 for about 15 minutes or until the pastry is crisp and golden.

LEEK, GOAT'S CHEESE AND SUN-DRIED TOMATO SAMOSAS V

If goat's cheese isn't your favourite, use a cheese such as Feta instead.

Makes about 24

about 10 sheets filo pastry (about 15 × 30cm/6 × 12 in)
about 50g (2 oz) butter, melted, for brushing

FILLING
25g (1 oz) butter
1 small leek (about 100g/4 oz), washed and finely sliced
50g (2 oz) crumbly goat's cheese, such as chèvre, in a roll
25g (1 oz) sun-dried tomatoes, drained from their oil and snipped into small pieces
salt and freshly ground black pepper

1 Melt the butter in a small pan. Add the leek and cook gently on the Simmering Plate until soft with a hint of colour. Allow to cool. Gently stir in the goat's cheese and sun-dried tomato, and season to taste.

2 Make up the little filo samosas as described in Prawn and Boursin Samosas, from stages 2–5. Bake in the same way as in stage 6. Store and freeze in the same way as well.

VEGETABLE SAMOSAS WITH GINGER AND LEMON V

Stir-fry the vegetables quickly so that they keep some crispness. These are similar to Chinese spring rolls, but in a samosa shape.

Makes about 24

about 10 sheets filo pastry (about 15 × 30cm/6 × 12 in) about 50g (2 oz) butter, melted, for brushing	FILLING 1 medium carrot 2 sticks celery 3 spring onions 1–2 tablespoons sunflower oil 1 × 1cm (½ in) piece of fresh root ginger, finely grated salt and freshly ground black pepper a squeeze of lemon juice

1 Cut the carrot, celery and spring onions into fine strips. Heat the oil in a large non-stick frying pan on the Boiling Plate, add the prepared vegetables and ginger, and stir-fry quickly until just tender – they should retain some bite. Season well, add a squeeze of lemon juice and leave to cool.

2 Make up the little filo samosas as described in Prawn and Boursin Samosas, from stages 2–5. Bake in the same way as in stage 6. Store and freeze in the same way as well.

POPPADUMS

Crisp and cook poppadums for your Indian supper by putting them directly on the Boiling Plate and gently lowering the lid. They're ready in seconds.

THE BEST PARMESAN BISCUITS V

Wonderful to go with drinks, or soup as a starter. They are a bit fiddly to make, so give yourself time, and you need to be in a patient mood!

Makes 65–70 tiny biscuits

75g (3 oz) Parmesan, freshly grated
50g (2 oz) butter, cut into small pieces
40g (1½ oz) plain flour

a generous pinch of English mustard
  powder
salt and freshly ground black pepper
a little extra Parmesan to sprinkle

1 Put all the measured ingredients into the processor with some salt and pepper, and blend until everything comes together. Chill if necessary, but usually you can roll out the pastry immediately.

2 Roll out very thinly, stamp into very small rounds, about 2.5cm (1 in) in diameter. Sprinkle the top of the biscuits with the extra Parmesan and arrange on Lift-Off paper on a baking sheet.

3 Slide on to the grid shelf on the floor of the Roasting Oven with the cold plain shelf on the second set of runners. Watch like a hawk as they take an amazingly short time to bake. Check after 3–4 minutes. Cool and enjoy!

TO PREPARE AHEAD   Make up to 2 weeks ahead and store in an airtight container. Refresh on a baking sheet in the Simmering Oven for a few minutes to crisp them up – but watch carefully!

TO FREEZE   Once cooked and cooled, pack in a polythene box between layers of kitchen paper. They will keep for about 1 month.

TO THAW   No need to thaw, just warm through in the Simmering Oven for a few minutes.

TO COOK IN A CONVENTIONAL OVEN   Cook in the oven preheated to 160°C/325°F/ Gas mark 3 for about 10–15 minutes.

MAIN COURSES

The main course is usually the centre of attraction in a meal, which is why this chapter is so long, containing as it does recipes for fish, poultry, game, meat, vegetarian and pasta dishes.

Fish is easy to cook on the Aga. Because the heat is so constant, a piece of fish can be seared, fried or poached in under 10 minutes. If you are wanting to keep fish hot, remember to under-cook it to begin with, otherwise it will be stringy, flavourless and lose all its juices. I love salmon, so there are quite a few recipes here. I've used some Thai spices in a couple of recipes – very up to the minute – and I've also included another version of my fish pie, which is such comforting food.

I've included a lot of chicken in the book, because I think chicken breasts are one of the best 'convenience' foods available, and chicken, as a white meat, is deemed healthier than red. (You could use thighs instead of breasts – the recipes are easy to adapt.) There are also a number of game recipes, ranging from my all-time favourite, pheasant (now readily available in supermarkets), to quail, guinea fowl and venison.

My meat recipes are new too, with a variety of international flavourings. Meat cooking on the Aga is very successful, primarily because you need to use so little fat, and slow-cooked dishes like the Kleftiko on page 109 are second to none. But I've also given you a selection of vegetarian main-course recipes, which are very up to date. I couldn't leave out pasta, either, especially as there are some very interesting flavours here, and I also include a delicious risotto. I think that there is something for everyone here.

AN EXCEEDINGLY GOOD FISH PIE

A very upmarket fish pie! When buying the fish, look out for special offers. If salmon fillet is more reasonable, use it instead.

Serves 6

75g (3 oz) butter

1 large onion, roughly chopped

50g (2 oz) plain flour

scant 600ml (20 fl oz) milk

salt and freshly ground black pepper

2 tablespoons lemon juice

700g (1½ lb) haddock or cod fillet, cut into 1cm (½ in) pieces

4 eggs, hard-boiled and roughly chopped

2 medium leeks, washed and thinly sliced

TOPPING

900g (2 lb) potatoes

about 8 tablespoons hot milk

50–75g (2–3 oz) butter

1 Grease a shallow 2.3 litre (80 fl oz) dish, using a little extra butter. Make the mashed potato topping as in the recipe on page 136.

2 Next make the sauce for the fish pie. Melt 50g (2 oz) of the butter in a medium pan on the Boiling Plate, and gently fry the onion until soft. Sprinkle in the flour then add the milk gradually, stirring well and allowing to thicken until all the milk has been included. Season, then add the lemon juice and the raw fish. Take off the heat, and pour into the prepared dish. Sprinkle over the egg, and leave to cool.

3 Melt the remaining butter in a frying pan on the Boiling Plate, add the leeks and stir-fry over a high heat until barely cooked through. Season. Arrange over the fish and sauce and press down a little. Spread the mashed potato over the mixture.

4 Cook in the Roasting Oven on the third set of runners for about 25 minutes until the potato topping is crisp and golden. Serve at once if possible.

TO PREPARE AHEAD   Prepare the pie to the end of stage 3. Cover with clingfilm and keep in the fridge for up to 24 hours before baking as directed.

TO FREEZE   Not suitable, because hard-boiled eggs and mashed potato do not freeze terribly well.

TO COOK IN A CONVENTIONAL OVEN   Cook the pie in the oven preheated to 180°C/350°F/Gas mark 4, for 30–35 minutes or until the potato is crisp and golden and the pie is piping hot.

BAKED SALMON WITH PARMESAN AND PARSLEY CRUST

This recipe is one of my all-time favourites, and is a perfect fish recipe to prepare ahead . It allows the sauce to become really cold and firm before oven baking. If it is a very special occasion and you like a lot of sauce, double up on the amount. I find that there is usually none left! A less rich sauce alternative follows this recipe.

Serves 6

6 × 150g (5 oz) salmon fillets, skinned
salt and freshly ground black pepper
butter if necessary
chopped fresh parsley

SAUCE
75ml (2½ fl oz) white wine
175g (6 oz) chestnut mushrooms, sliced
300ml (10 fl oz) double cream

TOPPING
25g (1 oz) fresh white breadcrumbs
25g (1 oz) Parmesan, coarsely grated
2 tablespoons chopped fresh parsley
grated rind of ½ lemon
paprika

1 Season both sides of the salmon fillets and place on Lift-Off paper on a baking sheet, or arrange in the large buttered roasting tin.

2 Measure the wine and mushrooms into a pan, and boil on the Boiling Plate for 1 minute. Lift out the mushrooms with a slotted spoon and reduce the wine to about 2 tablespoons. Add the cream, bring to the boil and reduce to a sauce consistency. Season. Return the mushrooms to the sauce and leave to cool completely.

3 Spoon a little of the cold mushroom mixture on each salmon fillet, but do not spread to the edge. Sprinkle the breadcrumbs, Parmesan, parsley and lemon rind on the mushroom mixture and dust with paprika. Leave in the fridge for 24 hours if necessary. Save the rest of the sauce, to reheat and serve separately.

4 Bake for 10–15 minutes on the grid shelf on the floor of the Roasting Oven. When the salmon is done, it will have changed from translucent to an opaque pink. Sprinkle with more chopped parsley and serve immediately.

continued overleaf

TO PREPARE AHEAD   Complete stages 2 and 3, cover with clingfilm and keep in the fridge for up to 24 hours.

TO FREEZE   Not suitable.

TO COOK IN A CONVENTIONAL OVEN   Cook in the oven preheated to 220°C/425°F/ Gas mark 7 for about 15 minutes.

ALTERNATIVE LIGHT MUSHROOM SAUCE

This is a less rich sauce if you prefer it. I go for the rich one every time!

Serves 6

175g (6 oz) chestnut mushrooms, sliced	1 level dessertspoon plain flour
juice of ½ lemon	1 × 200ml (7 fl oz) carton of low-fat crème fraîche

1 Cook the mushrooms in a saucepan on the Boiling Plate for 1 minute in the lemon juice.

2 Mix the flour with a little of the crème fraîche in a small bowl using a small whisk (this stabilises and thickens the crème fraîche when heated). Place the remaining crème fraîche in a saucepan and mix in the flour and crème fraîche mixture. Bring to the boil on the Boiling Plate, whisking all the time. When the sauce has thickened and just boiled, stir in the mushrooms and lemon juice and allow to cool completely.

3 Spread over the salmon as above, and sprinkle with the same topping.

GRILLING

Heavy cast-iron ridged grill pans take time to get really hot, so you can preheat them on the floor of the Roasting Oven until exceedingly hot. Make sure you use an oven glove to remove from the oven. And *don't* do this if your grill has a wooden handle, as it would spoil.

SEARED SALMON WITH LIME MUSTARD DRESSING

Use salmon tail or middle cut fillets, and choose size to suit appetites. Cut the fillets in half lengthways to give as a starter.

Serves 4

4 × 150g (5 oz) fresh salmon tail
    fillets, skin on
salt and freshly ground black pepper
olive oil
a few lettuce leaves

DRESSING
1 generous teaspoon coarse grain
    mustard
3 teaspoons caster sugar
juice of 2 limes
4 tablespoons olive oil
2 tomatoes, skinned and seeded

1 Heat the grill pan until piping hot on the Boiling Plate or in the Roasting Oven (see opposite).

2 Season the salmon, toss in olive oil, and put gently, flesh side down, on to the hot grill pan and cook for 30–45 seconds. Turn on to the skin side and continue cooking for about 2 minutes. Draw the pan off the heat and leave the fish to cook in the residual heat of the pan until done.

3 Make the dressing by measuring all the ingredients, except the tomatoes, into a clean jam jar. Add salt and pepper and give it a good shake. Slice the skinned tomatoes into thin strips and mix with the dressing.

4 Serve the warm salmon on a bed of lettuce with a little dressing poured over.

TO PREPARE AHEAD Make the dressing ahead. Cook the fish as needed.

TO FREEZE Not suitable.

TO COOK IN A CONVENTIONAL OVEN Cook the fish on a grill pan on the hob in the normal way.

THAI SALMON

This truly simple recipe evolved from an idea passed on to me in the time-honoured fashion of a few scribbles on the back of an old envelope.

Timing is all-important here. As Marco Pierre White said in his interview with Sue Lawley on Desert Island Discs, one of the reasons he did not allow any conversation between staff in his kitchen was that 5 seconds too long could ruin the cooking of a piece of fish.

Red Thai curry paste is available from good delicatessens and supermarkets, where it is usually to be found on the herbs and spices shelf. I have suggested a scant teaspoon of the Thai paste, but add more if you like.

Serves 4

2 × 275g (10 oz) fresh salmon tail fillets, skin left on
olive oil
salt and freshly ground black pepper

SAUCE
1 × 2.5cm (1 in) piece of fresh root ginger
1 tablespoon olive oil
1 small clove garlic, crushed
1 small orange
1 scant teaspoon red Thai curry paste
300ml (10 fl oz) crème fraîche

1 Cut each salmon fillet in half lengthways, brush both sides with oil, and season.

2 Using a potato peeler, peel the ginger and cut into needle-thin strips lengthways. Soften in the oil in a large-based pan on the Simmering Plate for a minute, then add the garlic. Stir well, cover, and transfer to the floor of the Simmering Oven for 10 minutes. (The reason for using a large pan is that it is quicker to reduce the sauce later.)

3 Remove the rind from the orange using a zester, then squeeze the juice. Add the Thai paste to the ginger and garlic mixture, stir well and then add the orange juice and zest and lastly the crème fraîche. Bring to the boil on the Boiling Plate, simmer for 2–3 minutes, and add salt to taste. If necessary, boil further to reduce to a creamy consistency. Keep warm.

4 Put a ridged grill pan to heat up on the Simmering Plate. Transfer to the Boiling Plate. Put the salmon, flesh side down, on to the hot grill pan and cook for 30–45 seconds, then turn on to the skin side and continue cooking for about $3\frac{1}{2}$ minutes (about $3\frac{1}{2}$–5 minutes total), according to the thickness of the salmon. Watch it like a hawk. (If you like your fish barely cooked, do not be tempted to leave it longer, as you can always return it to the pan, but there is nothing you can do if it is over-cooked.)

5 To serve, pour a little warm sauce on to each plate, place a fillet of salmon to one side of it, and then serve the rest of the sauce separately.

TO PREPARE AHEAD   Thai salmon is best grilled to order. Make the sauce ahead. Cool, cover and refrigerate.

TO FREEZE   Not suitable. Salmon is best cooked to serve so that the skin stays crisp.

TO REHEAT   Reheat the sauce gently on the Simmering Plate.

TO COOK IN A CONVENTIONAL OVEN   Use the hob to make the sauce, simmering gently. Heat the ridged grill pan over a high heat and cook the salmon as desired.

FRESH SALMON AND HERB FISH CAKES

The fish cakes are oven baked with no additional butter other than a generous greasing of the oven tray. They freeze well before cooking and can be eaten for breakfast, lunch or supper! You can fry the fish cakes in a little oil and butter if preferred. They are delicious served with a tartare sauce (see opposite).

Serves 6-8

550g (1¼ lb) potatoes, Desirée or King Edwards, peeled weight	3 heaped tablespoons chopped fresh parsley
salt and freshly ground black pepper	1 heaped tablespoon chopped fresh dill
450g (1 lb) fresh skinless salmon fillets	
about 50g (2 oz) butter	2 drops Tabasco sauce
2 good tablespoons light mayonnaise	fresh white breadcrumbs

1 Cut the potatoes into even sizes and boil in salted water on the Boiling Plate for 5 minutes. Drain, cover and transfer to the Simmering Oven until tender, about 40 minutes. Drain any excess water created, and mash with the buttery juices from the fish when it is cooked.

2 About 15 minutes before the potatoes finish cooking, season the fish with salt and pepper. Cut the fillets in half if they are large. Wrap the fish in a foil parcel with a good 30g (1¼ oz) butter. Bake on the grid shelf on the floor of the Roasting Oven for 10–12 minutes or until the fish is opaque and flakes in the centre when tested with a fork.

3 Flake the fish into a bowl with the mashed potatoes, discarding any bones. Add the mayonnaise, herbs and Tabasco. Taste the mixture and season well with salt and pepper. Allow the mixture to cool, then put into the fridge until firm enough to shape.

4 Divide the mixture into twelve even-sized round fish cakes and roll in breadcrumbs. Cover and chill if time allows.

5 Preheat a baking sheet covered with a piece of Lift-Off paper on the floor of the Roasting Oven for 5 minutes. Generously butter the hot Lift-Off paper using kitchen paper. Bake the fish cakes for 4 minutes, turn over and bake for a further 4 minutes until golden brown and piping hot. (If you don't preheat the baking sheet the fish cakes are apt to spread.)

6 If need be, the fish cakes can be kept warm for up to 40 minutes in the Simmering Oven. Serve with Light Tartare Sauce (see opposite) and lemon wedges. They are also delicious just on their own with, say, broccoli and peas.

TO PREPARE AHEAD   Prepare the fish cakes ahead to the end of stage 4. Cover with clingfilm and store in the fridge for up to 2 days.

TO FREEZE   Open-freeze the prepared fish cakes at the end of stage 4 until solid, then transfer to a freezer bag and freeze for up to 4 months.

TO THAW   Remove the fish cakes from the freezer bag and put in a single layer on a baking tray. Cover and thaw for 3 hours at room temperature or overnight in the fridge.

TO COOK IN A CONVENTIONAL OVEN   Bake the parcel of fish in the oven, preheated to 200°C/400°F/Gas mark 6 for 12–15 minutes until the fish is opaque and flakes easily. Make and shape the fish cakes as above. Preheat a heavy baking sheet in the oven. Lightly grease with butter and put the fish cakes in a single layer, brush with melted butter, then cook at 220°C/425°F/Gas mark 7 for 20 minutes until crisp, golden and hot through.

LIGHT TARTARE SAUCE

Using a light mayonnaise and crème fraîche makes this tartare sauce much lighter to eat – and less fattening!

Serves 6–8

4 tablespoons chopped fresh parsley	salt and freshly ground black pepper
4 tablespoons crème fraîche	juice of ½ lime or lemon
4 tablespoons light mayonnaise	
4 spring onions, chopped	

1 Simply mix all of the above ingredients together.

MONKFISH PROVENÇALE WITH CRISP BACON LARDONS

These firm fish fillets, with their Mediterranean sauce, are very good served with rice and perhaps a green salad.

Serves 4

4 × 150g (5 oz) monkfish tail fillets, skinned

8 rashers smoked streaky bacon, snipped into thin strips

salt and freshly ground black pepper

1 tablespoon olive oil

2 tablespoons chopped fresh parsley

TOMATO HERB SAUCE

1 tablespoon olive oil

1 onion, chopped

2–3 cloves garlic, crushed

1 × 400g (14 oz) tin of chopped tomatoes

2 tablespoons sun-dried tomato paste

1 teaspoon chopped fresh tarragon

1 teaspoon balsamic vinegar

a pinch of caster sugar to taste

1 First make the sauce. Heat the oil in a large frying pan on the Boiling Plate, add the onion and garlic, and fry gently for 3–4 minutes, stirring from time to time. Cover and transfer to the floor of the Simmering Oven for 10 minutes, until the onion is soft. Return to the Boiling Plate, and add the tomatoes, tomato paste, tarragon, vinegar, salt, pepper and sugar, and bring back to the boil. Turn into an ovenproof serving dish large enough to hold the fish in one layer.

2 Meanwhile cook the snipped bacon in a pan on the floor of the Roasting Oven for about 10 minutes until crisp, shaking from time to time.

3 Ensure all the stiff white membrane has been removed from the fish, then season with salt and black pepper. Heat the oil in a pan on the Boiling Plate and quickly fry the monkfish on all sides until golden brown, making sure it is not quite cooked through completely. Lay the tails on the tomato herb sauce.

4 Slide the fish serving dish on to the grid shelf on the floor of the Roasting Oven and cook, uncovered, for about 15 minutes until piping hot.

5 Remove from the oven, sprinkle with warm crispy bacon and chopped parsley, and serve immediately.

TO PREPARE AHEAD   Prepare to the end of stage 3 up to 6 hours ahead. Cover and keep in the fridge.

TO FREEZE   Freeze the sauce only for about 6 weeks.

TO THAW   Thaw for about 4 hours at room temperature.

TO REHEAT   Follow stage 4. Reheat the bacon in the Simmering Oven for 5–10 minutes.

TO COOK IN A CONVENTIONAL OVEN   Make the sauce on the hob in the usual way. Cook the monkfish with the sauce as in stage 4 in the oven preheated to 200°C/400°F/Gas mark 6 for 15–20 minutes until piping hot.

FILLETS OF TROUT WITH DILL AND CUCUMBER

Although I have used skinned trout fillets, you could use sole fillets instead. This is a wonderful dish in summer, the dill lending an incomparable flavour.

Serves 4

½ cucumber
25g (1 oz) butter
4 × 375–400g (12–14 oz) trout, skinned, boned and opened out
1 medium bunch of fresh dill, chopped (leave a few sprigs whole to garnish)

salt and freshly ground black pepper
juice of 1 lemon

SAUCE
200ml (7 fl oz) crème fraîche
a little lemon juice

1 Peel the cucumber then cut in half lengthways. Remove the seeds using a melon scoop or teaspoon, and cut into slices about 5mm (¼ in) thick, making a series of horseshoe shapes. Sauté the cucumber in the butter on the Boiling Plate for 2 minutes.

2 Grease an ovenproof baking dish or the small roasting tin and place the trout in it, skinned side down. Divide two-thirds of the cucumber between the four trout, and sprinkle some chopped dill on to each one. (Reserve some chopped dill for the crème fraîche.) Season with salt and pepper and pour over the lemon juice. Fold the fillets back over the cucumber and dill, and put the rest of the cucumber over and round them. Cover with foil.

3 Slide the tin into the Roasting Oven on the second set of runners. Bake the trout for 10–15 minutes until the flesh has turned pale pink and is opaque.

4 Stir the remaining chopped dill into the crème fraîche with a little lemon juice and some seasoning. Keep in the fridge until ready to serve the trout.

5 Put each trout on a warmed plate, and put a generous dessertspoonful of the dill crème fraîche beside it. (You could hand the sauce round in a bowl separately.) Decorate with sprigs of dill and serve with new potatoes and mangetout.

TO PREPARE AHEAD   The trout can be prepared ahead in the morning, ready to be cooked in the evening. Completely cool the sautéed cucumber at the end of stage 1, then complete to the end of stage 2. Cover and keep in the fridge until ready to cook.

TO FREEZE   Not suitable.

TO COOK IN A CONVENTIONAL OVEN   Bake the trout in the oven preheated to 180°C/350°F/ Gas mark 4 for about 20–25 minutes until the fish is opaque.

OVEN-GRILLED DOVER SOLE AND OTHER FISH

At last I have found the Aga answer to grilled Dover sole, especially for more than two fish. You can use the same method for other unskinned sole and plaice, or fish cutlets and steaks. Great news too – you can part-cook them ahead with success every time, then reheat later.

Allow 1 sole per person

butter, softened
whole Dover soles, skinned

salt and freshly ground black pepper

1 Melt some butter in either the large or small roasting tin in the Roasting Oven – the size of tin depends on how many soles you are cooking. Use enough butter to give a thin layer over the base of the tin.

2 Preheat an ungreased grill pan either on the floor of the Roasting Oven or on the Boiling Plate until very very hot. (Take great care to use an oven glove if heating the pan in the oven, as the handle of course becomes exceedingly hot.)

3 Spread the soles on the fattest side with soft butter. Place the hot grill pan on the Boiling Plate. Take each sole and lightly press the buttered side on to the grill pan so that brown grid marks appear on the sole. This will take 1 or 2 minutes. Dip the fish in the melted butter, season and lie in the buttered tin grilled side uppermost. Place the tin on the floor of the Roasting Oven for 8–12 minutes until the fish are done.

4 Serve immediately.

TO PREPARE AHEAD   Grill the sole on one side, put in the roasting tin in butter as in stage 3, and put in the fridge. Do this in the morning and serve in the evening.

TO FREEZE   Not suitable.

TO REHEAT   Place on the floor of the Roasting Oven for about 10–13 minutes.

TO COOK IN A CONVENTIONAL OVEN   Use grill.

SEARED FILLET OF SEA BASS WITH TOMATO AND AVOCADO SALSA

If liked, the salsa may be served hot. Take care only to bring it to piping hot, do not cook it.

Serves 4

4 × 150g (5 oz) fillets of sea bass or red mullet, skin on	1 large clove garlic, cut into 8
olive oil	1 bunch of parsley stalks
sea salt and freshly ground black pepper	a few basil stalks
a handful of fresh basil leaves, shredded at the last moment	1 large avocado, a fraction under-ripe
	1 lime, halved
	2 tomatoes, skinned, seeded and cut into thin strips
SALSA	2 teaspoons capers (optional)
4 tablespoons olive oil	1 teaspoon caster sugar
2 tablespoons water	
1 shallot, quartered	

1 For the salsa, put the oil, water, shallot, garlic, parsley and basil stalks into a small pan with some salt and pepper. Cover and place in the Simmering Oven for 20 minutes to allow the flavours to infuse. Strain, then cool.

2 Peel the avocado and cut it in half. Remove the stone, place the cut side of the avocado down on a board and cut in slices, then toss in the juice of one lime half. Add the tomato strips, capers (if using), avocado and sugar to the infused olive oil mixture. Season.

3 Lightly brush the fish fillets with olive oil and season with sea salt and pepper. Preheat a ridged grill pan, first on the Simmering Plate, then the Boiling Plate until piping hot. Lay the fillets flesh side down on to the hot grill pan and cook for 45 seconds, then turn on to the skin side, cover the pan with a lid, and continue cooking for about 4–5 minutes, depending on the thickness of the fish. (It is better to under-cook as it can be returned to the pan, but there is no remedy for over-cooked fish.)

4 Place the fillets on four plates, spoon the salsa to one side of the fish and garnish with shredded leaves of basil and wedges cut from the remaining half lime.

TO PREPARE AHEAD Best made and served immediately.

TO FREEZE Not suitable.

TO COOK IN A CONVENTIONAL OVEN Cook on the hob in the usual way.

THAI PRAWNS WITH CORIANDER AND NOODLES

A wonderfully healthy supper dish, very tasty and impressive with the large prawns. Don't forget to serve finger bowls with this dish: it may be great fun to peel the prawns as you eat them, but it's a bit messy! Chinese egg noodles need a very short cooking time; check the packet instructions. To bruise the lemongrass, gently crush with a rolling pin. You need to work quickly with this recipe, with all the ingredients to hand.

Serves 4

2 tablespoons sunflower oil	I dessertspoon red Thai curry paste
I small onion, chopped	(less if you don't like it hot!)
2 cloves garlic, crushed	2 tablespoons hoisin sauce, or to taste
I small hot red chilli, seeded and	I × 250g (9 oz) packet of medium
thinly sliced	Chinese egg noodles
I stem lemongrass, cut in half and bruised	225g (8 oz) large raw shelled tiger prawns
I × 4cm (1½ in) piece of fresh root	100g (4 oz) large raw prawns in shells,
ginger, peeled and grated	heads on (optional)
juice of I lime	225g (8 oz) baby spinach, roughly chopped
2 tablespoons soy sauce	salt and freshly ground black pepper
	I small bunch of fresh coriander, chopped

1 Heat the oil in a large non-stick frying pan on the Boiling Plate. Add the onion, garlic, chilli, lemongrass and ginger, and stir-fry for 2–3 minutes.

2 Mix together the lime juice, soy sauce, curry paste and hoisin sauce in a bowl.

3 Cook the egg noodles in boiling salted water on the Boiling Plate according to the packet directions (usually 4 minutes).

4 Add all the prawns to the frying pan and stir-fry for about a minute. Add the spinach and continue to stir-fry until the prawns are pink, about 3–4 minutes.

5 Discard the lemongrass and drain the noodles. Add the noodles and lime juice mixture to the spinach mixture and toss. Season lightly with salt and pepper. Heat through for 1 minute and serve immediately sprinkled with chopped coriander.

TO PREPARE AHEAD   Just prepare all the vegetables, have all the other ingredients ready and make as needed.

TO FREEZE   Not suitable.

TO COOK IN A CONVENTIONAL OVEN   Use the hob in the normal way.

WATERCROFT CHICKEN

A great recipe for entertaining, as much of the work can be done well in advance. You can also adapt the recipe for quail (see page 88).

Serves 6

6 boned chicken breasts, skin on
2 tablespoons lime marmalade
25g (1 oz) butter
salt and freshly ground black pepper

MUSHROOM FARCE
15g (½ oz) butter
2 shallots, finely chopped
150g (5 oz) button mushrooms, finely chopped

25g (1 oz) breadcrumbs
1 small egg, beaten (you may not need all of it)

SAUCE
1 × 200ml (7 fl oz) carton of crème fraîche
juice of 1 lime
lots of chopped fresh parsley

1 For the mushroom farce, melt the butter in a pan on the Boiling Plate, add the shallot and cook for about a minute. Cover and transfer to the floor of the Simmering Oven for 10 minutes. Add the mushrooms, toss quickly in the butter and shallot mixture and cook for another 2 minutes on the Boiling Plate. Remove from the heat, add the breadcrumbs and egg, and season well (do not add all the egg if it seems too wet). Leave to cool.

2 Put the marmalade into a small saucepan and heat very gently on the Simmering Plate. As it begins to dissolve, add the butter and stir well until it is all combined.

3 To stuff the chicken breasts, carefully lift the skin down one side and, using a teaspoon, push the mushroom farce underneath, then fold back. Put the six chicken breasts into the large greased roasting tin, season and spoon the butter and marmalade mixture over the top.

4 Cook in the Roasting Oven in the highest position for about 15 minutes until golden brown and the chicken is just cooked through. Transfer the chicken to a warmed serving dish using a slotted spoon and put into the Simmering Oven while making the sauce.

5 To make the sauce, scrape all the bits from the base and sides of the roasting tin, add the crème fraîche and lime juice and stir well. Return to the floor of the Roasting Oven for 5 minutes. Let the sauce bubble, stir well then add parsley, season to taste and serve with the chicken. Some radicchio or chicory would make a good garnish.

TO PREPARE AHEAD Make the stuffing ahead of time and cool. Stuff the chicken breasts, cover and refrigerate, up to 24 hours ahead. Do not glaze until ready to cook.

TO FREEZE Freeze the raw, stuffed chicken breasts for up to 6 months.

TO THAW Defrost for about 4–6 hours at room temperature.

TO COOK IN A CONVENTIONAL OVEN Bake the chicken in the preheated oven at 190°C/375°F/Gas mark 5 for about 20 minutes until the chicken is tender. Then make the sauce from the juices in the roasting tin.

GARLIC-STUFFED CHICKEN WITH THYME AND CHIVES

Take care not to over-cook the chicken, otherwise it will lose its moisture and flavour and the bright green of the herbs will fade. This serves six as a hot main course, or ten if serving cold as part of a buffet or picnic.

Serves 6

6 boned chicken breasts, skin on
salt and freshly ground black pepper
butter

STUFFING
a good knob of butter
1 medium onion, chopped
225g (8 oz) full-fat soft cheese
1 good tablespoon mixed chopped fresh
   chives and thyme
2 fat cloves garlic, crushed
1 egg yolk
a little grated nutmeg

1 Melt the butter for the stuffing in a small pan and sauté the onion for 5 minutes on the Simmering Plate. Cover and transfer to the Simmering Oven for 10 minutes or so until tender.

2 Turn the onion into a bowl, allow to cool slightly, then mix with all the other stuffing ingredients. Mash down and season well.

3 Place the chicken breasts on a board, skin side uppermost. Loosen the skin from one side. Stuff a sixth of the cheese mixture into this pocket and replace the skin. Do the same with the other five breasts.

4 Arrange the chicken in a buttered and seasoned large roasting tin and brush with melted butter. Roast in the Roasting Oven, on the highest set of runners, for about 15 minutes until just done. If the chicken is getting too brown, transfer to the floor of the Roasting Oven.

5 Serve hot, warm or cold, cut in diagonal slices. If serving hot, strain off any juices in the tin and make a good thin gravy, adding a little reduced white wine and cream if liked.

TO PREPARE AHEAD   Make the cheese and herb stuffing mixture and allow to cool completely. Complete to the end of stage 3. Cover and keep in the fridge for up to 12 hours.

TO FREEZE   Prepare the chicken to the end of stage 3, cooling the cheese and herb mixture thoroughly before stuffing the chicken. Wrap and freeze for up to 6 months.

TO THAW   Thaw at room temperature for 8 hours, or overnight in the fridge.

TO COOK IN A CONVENTIONAL OVEN   Cook the chicken in the oven, preheated to 190°C/375°F/Gas mark 5 for 25–30 minutes, until the chicken is cooked through.

MARINATED SUMMER CHICKEN

Roast a chicken or turkey in the Aga in the normal way, then use the meat from the chicken or leftovers from the turkey in this light, easy summer dish, to be served cold.

Serves 8

the meat from a 1.4kg (3 lb) cooked chicken, without skin or bone, or 450g (1 lb) cooked turkey, without skin or bone
salt and freshly ground black pepper
1 × 200ml (7 fl oz) carton of crème fraîche
225g (8 oz) seedless grapes, plus a few extra to garnish
25g (1 oz) pine kernels, toasted for 2–4 minutes (see page 83)
rocket or flat-leaf parsley

MARINADE
1 generous tablespoon coarse grain mustard
3 tablespoons olive oil
juice of 2 lemons
3 teaspoons caster sugar
3 spring onions, finely sliced

1   Cut the cooked chicken or turkey into bite-sized pieces.

2   Measure all the marinade ingredients (keeping back 2 tablespoons of lemon juice for the grapes) into a jam jar and shake well. Mix the marinade with the chicken or turkey, season well and leave to marinate overnight.

3   Before serving, stir in the crème fraîche and halved grapes tossed in the remaining lemon juice, and sprinkle over the toasted pine kernels.

4   Garnish with the extra grapes and some rocket leaves or parsley.

TO PREPARE AHEAD   Simply follow the recipe, which means you are a day ahead.

TO FREEZE   Not suitable.

SPATCHCOCK POUSSINS IN SAGE AND ORANGE MARINADE

One poussin is often too much for one person, so I cut them in half once cooked and offer half to begin with, and then possibly the other half for seconds. Or use chicken breasts if you prefer.

Serves 6

4 poussins, about 400g (14 oz) each	1 tablespoon olive oil
a few sprigs of fresh sage	2 tablespoons soy sauce
	1 tablespoon dried sage
MARINADE	1 dessertspoon coarsely grated fresh
300ml (10 fl oz) carton orange juice	root ginger
2 cloves garlic, crushed	salt and freshly ground black pepper

1 First cut the back bones out of the poussins, using good kitchen scissors or shears.

2 Put one large freezer bag inside another. Combine the marinade ingredients and put with the poussins into the inner bag. Marinate for about 24 hours in the fridge.

3 Take the poussins out of the marinade and save the latter. Arrange the poussins, skin side up, in the large roasting tin. Flatten the poussins by pressing down with the heel of your hand on the breast bone. The wings will sit neatly, and then tuck the legs up to the thigh. Snip off the bony leg joint at the end of the drumstick.

4 Hang the tin on the top set of runners in the Roasting Oven and roast for 20 minutes. Pour the marinade over the poussins and return to the oven for 5–10 minutes.

5 Remove the tin from the oven and cut the poussins in half down the breast bone. Strain the juices, and reheat on the Boiling Plate. Check the seasoning and serve the sauce separately. Decorate with the sprigs of sage.

TO PREPARE AHEAD You are already, by marinating the poussins for 24 hours in the fridge.

TO FREEZE At stage 5, cool and freeze, meat and sauce separately, for up to 2 months.

TO THAW Thaw for about 6 hours at room temperature.

TO REHEAT Reheat in the Roasting Oven with the sauce for 15 minutes.

TO COOK IN A CONVENTIONAL OVEN Cook in the oven preheated to 200°C/400°F/ Gas mark 6 for about 40–45 minutes or until cooked through.

CHICKEN CASSOULET

The word 'cassoulet' comes from 'casserole', the earthenware pot in which this French stew is cooked. This is a modern lighter version of the traditional recipe.

Serves 4

1 tablespoon chopped fresh thyme	75g (3 oz) pancetta, diced
6 teaspoons sun-dried tomato paste	150ml (5 fl oz) white wine
4 chicken breasts, skinned	1 × 400g (14 oz) tin of chopped tomatoes
salt and freshly ground black pepper	1 × 400g (14 oz) tin of butter beans,
2 tablespoons olive oil	drained and rinsed
1 onion, finely chopped	1 tablespoon chopped fresh parsley
2 cloves garlic, crushed	1 tablespoon chopped fresh chives or
½–1 red chilli, seeded and sliced	spring onion tops

1 Mix half the thyme leaves with 4 teaspoons of the sun-dried tomato paste, and spread a teaspoonful on each chicken breast. Season the chicken well.

2 Place the chicken breasts in the roasting tin on the roasting rack, and hang the tin from the top set of runners in the Roasting Oven. Roast for 15 minutes, then transfer to the Simmering Oven for 10 minutes to allow the chicken to relax.

3 To make the bean sauce, heat the olive oil in a large frying pan on the Boiling Plate, add the onion, garlic and chilli, and fry for a few minutes, stirring from time to time. Cover and transfer to the Simmering Oven for about 10 minutes, until the onion is soft.

4 Return to the Boiling Plate, add the pancetta and fry to brown it. Mix the wine, tomatoes and remaining tomato paste together, add to the pan and boil rapidly until the pan is nearly dry. Stir in the beans, the parsley, remaining thyme and seasoning.

5 A few minutes before serving warm through the bean sauce and divide between four plates. Sprinkle with chopped chives or spring onion tops. Carve each chicken breast on the diagonal, and place on the bean sauce. Serve immediately.

TO PREPARE AHEAD   The bean sauce can be chilled for 2 days if necessary.

TO FREEZE   Not suitable.

TO REHEAT   Complete to stage 2 whilst the sauce is reheating, then continue as above.

TO COOK IN A CONVENTIONAL OVEN   Roast the chicken at 220°C/425°F/Gas mark 7 for about 15 minutes. Make the sauce on the hob.

DEVILLED CHICKEN

This recipe couldn't be easier, and it's very popular with the young. It would be good, perhaps, for supper in the kitchen.

Serves 6

12 chicken thighs, skinned
salt and freshly ground black pepper

SAUCE
1 rounded tablespoon apricot jam
1 teaspoon Dijon mustard
a good pinch of cayenne pepper
1 large clove garlic, crushed
1 tablespoon Worcestershire sauce
3 tablespoons tomato ketchup
1 tablespoon soy sauce

1 Season the chicken thighs well on all sides and put in the roasting tin, well greased and seasoned.

2 Measure the jam into a basin, add the mustard, cayenne, garlic and Worcestershire sauce, and blend well until smooth. Add the other ingredients, season with black pepper and a little salt, and pour over the chicken, coating evenly.

3 Slide the roasting tin on to the top set of runners in the Roasting Oven and cook for about 15 minutes until golden brown. To test when the chicken is done, prod the thickest part with a fine skewer. If the juices run out clear, the chicken is done; if pink, give the chicken a little longer.

4 Serve hot with rice and a green salad.

TO PREPARE AHEAD   Complete to the end of stage 2. Cover and refrigerate for about 8 hours.

TO FREEZE   Prepare to the end of stage 2 and freeze for up to 3 months.

TO THAW   Thaw for 4–6 hours at room temperature.

TO COOK IN A CONVENTIONAL OVEN   Cook in the oven, preheated to 190°C/375°F/Gas mark 5 for about 20–30 minutes until cooked through and golden brown. Turn half way through cooking.

CHICKEN WITH MADEIRA AND TARRAGON SAUCE

This recipe also works well with guinea fowl or young pheasants. Tarragon is particularly good here. Make sure you find French rather than Russian tarragon, as the latter is not nearly so flavourful.

Serves 4

40g (1½ oz) butter	100ml (4 fl oz) Madeira
1 tablespoon sunflower oil	salt and freshly ground black pepper
8 chicken thighs, skinned	1 × 200ml (7 fl oz) carton of crème fraîche
225g (8 oz) shallots, finely chopped	
25g (1 oz) plain flour	1 scant tablespoon chopped fresh tarragon
300ml (10 fl oz) chicken stock	

1 Put the butter and oil in a large non-stick frying pan on the Boiling Plate, and brown the chicken thighs until golden. Lift out of the pan and put to the side. Add the shallots to the frying pan and brown quickly. Lift out and put with the chicken. Transfer the pan to the Simmering Plate.

2 Blend the flour into the fat and juices remaining in the pan. Slowly add the stock and then the Madeira. Season well, and return the chicken joints and shallots to the pan. Bring to the boil on the Boiling Plate, cover and transfer to the floor of the Simmering Oven until tender, about 35 minutes.

3 Arrange the chicken on a serving dish and keep warm. Skim off any fat from the sauce, add the crème fraîche and bring back to the boil on the Boiling Plate. Check the seasoning and add the tarragon. Pour the sauce over the chicken and sprinkle with a little more tarragon.

TO PREPARE AHEAD   Not necessary.

TO FREEZE   Cook and cool the chicken, then freeze in a freezer container for up to 3 months. Freeze the sauce separately in a small pot for the same time.

TO THAW   Thaw for about 4 hours at room temperature.

TO REHEAT   Put the chicken thighs in the roasting tin, slide into the top of the Roasting Oven, and heat for about 8–10 minutes. Reheat the sauce in a pan on the Boiling Plate until hot right through.

TO COOK IN A CONVENTIONAL OVEN   Cook in the oven, preheated to 190°C/375°F/Gas mark 5 for about 20–25 minutes until cooked through.

CHICKEN LIVERS WITH TOASTED PINE KERNELS

For an even speedier dish buy a packet of prepared mixed leaf salad at the supermarket. Toast the pine kernels in a non-stick pan on the Simmering Plate until pale golden. Don't risk the oven! They are delicious added to the dish while still piping hot.

Serves 6 as a starter, or 4 as a lunch or supper dish

450g (1 lb) fresh chicken livers
  (usually 2 tubs or packets)
175g (6 oz) thick rashers streaky bacon,
  rinded and cut into 5mm (¼ in) strips
3 thick slices of white bread, crusts
  removed, cubed
1 tablespoon olive oil
100g (4 oz) button mushrooms,
  coarsely sliced

4 tablespoons salad dressing
3 whole Little Gem lettuces
6 firm tomatoes, each cut into 5–7 slices
salt and freshly ground black pepper
25g (1 oz) butter
2 tablespoons balsamic vinegar
40g (1½ oz) pine kernels, toasted
  (see above)
chopped sage or parsley

1 Drain the chicken livers in a sieve over a bowl. Using a pair of kitchen scissors, halve the larger pieces and remove any stringy bits.

2 Soften the bacon in a large non-stick frying pan on the Boiling Plate, then cook quickly until brown. Lift out with a slotted spoon and keep hot. Add the bread croûtons to the pan, adding a little olive oil if necessary, and fry until crisp and brown. Keep hot.

3 Toss the sliced mushrooms in the dressing until coated. Arrange 5–7 lettuce leaves in a circle on each plate. Make an inner circle using 5–7 slices of tomato on each. Season and arrange the mushrooms over the tomatoes and drizzle the remaining dressing over the lettuce leaves.

4 Heat the butter in a frying pan on the Boiling Plate until sizzling and really hot, add the chicken livers and cook them, turning frequently, for about 2 minutes. Add the bacon and croûtons and toss until hot and crispy, then spoon into the middle of the six portions of salad.

5 Deglaze the pan with the balsamic vinegar and pour over the livers. Sprinkle on the toasted pine kernels and decorate with sage or parsley. Serve immediately.

TO PREPARE AHEAD Make the croûtons ahead. To reheat, add to the frying pan at stage 2 once the bacon has become crisp.

TO FREEZE Not suitable

TO COOK IN A CONVENTIONAL OVEN Cook on the hob in the normal way.

TURKEY CHIN CHOW

A very different turkey recipe using leftover turkey from the Christmas Day roast. The turkey must be as fresh as possible.

Serves 4

1 x 425g (15 oz) tin of coconut milk
1 tablespoon cornflour
2 tablespoons soy sauce
4 tablespoons hoisin sauce
1 x 227g (8 oz) tin of water chestnuts, drained and halved
4 spring onions, sliced on the diagonal (keep the white and green parts separate)

1 x 5cm (2 in) piece of fresh root ginger, peeled and finely grated
salt and freshly ground black pepper
350g (12 oz) freshly cooked turkey, cut into bite-sized pieces
1 red pepper, seeded and finely sliced lengthways

1 Pour the coconut milk into a medium pan on the Simmering Plate, and blend in the cornflour, soy sauce and hoisin sauce. Bring up to the boil, stirring, and allow to thicken. Stir in the water chestnuts, the white part of the spring onions and the ginger. Season well, then add the turkey and red pepper.

2 Return to simmering point then turn into a shallow ovenproof dish. Slide on to the grid shelf on the floor of the Roasting Oven and bake for about 15 minutes until piping hot.

3 Remove from the oven, sprinkle with the reserved green spring onion tops, and serve immediately with basmati or red rice and salad.

TO PREPARE AHEAD Have the ingredients ready chopped and then it is extremely quick to cook.

TO FREEZE Not suitable.

TO COOK IN A CONVENTIONAL OVEN Cook at 190°C/375°F/Gas mark 5 for about 20 minutes until piping hot.

RED-HOT TURKEY

This is a wonderful dish using up leftover, cooked turkey. It must be really fresh, not the very last of the leftovers, as the cooking time is short. It is a spicy hot version of Hot American Chicken, which is in my original Aga book, and is a very popular recipe.

Serves 4–6

150ml (5 fl oz) low-calorie mayonnaise	6 medium sticks celery, sliced
2 heaped tablespoons Greek yoghurt	4 spring onions, finely sliced
4 tablespoons red pesto	50g (2 oz) Parmesan, grated
4 tablespoons sun-dried tomato paste	freshly ground black pepper
350g (12 oz) cooked turkey or	a few potato crisps, crumbled
chicken, diced	a little paprika

1 Combine the mayonnaise, yoghurt, red pesto sauce and sun-dried tomato paste in a large bowl and mix well. Add the turkey or chicken, celery, spring onions and about half the grated Parmesan. Season with black pepper and blend together, then turn the mixture into a shallow ovenproof dish. Sprinkle with the remaining cheese and crushed crisps, and dust lightly with paprika.

2 Bake on the grid shelf in the centre of the Roasting Oven for about 10 minutes until hot right through but not boiling. The sauce may separate if you cook it for any longer.

3 Serve straightaway with a green salad.

TO PREPARE AHEAD   Prepare as indicated in stage 1, sprinkling with the cheese but not the crisps. Cover and keep in the fridge up to 24 hours ahead. Sprinkle with the crisps and dust with paprika just before cooking.

TO FREEZE   Not suitable.

TO COOK IN A CONVENTIONAL OVEN   Cook in the oven, preheated to 220°C/425°F/ Gas mark 7, for 10–15 minutes until hot right through. Take care not to over-cook or the sauce may separate.

HURLEY DUCK BREASTS

Why Hurley? Lucy, my assistant of ten years, lived in Hurley, and it is her invention. Canned mango is surprisingly good, but take care to add it at the very end as it breaks up easily. This recipe does not use the skin of the duck. I render down the skins in the small roasting tin in the Simmering Oven overnight. By this time the skins are crisp, and you have plenty of duck fat which is wonderful to use for crisp roast potatoes.

Serves 4–6

4–6 duck breasts	3 tablespoons brandy
50g (2 oz) toasted flaked almonds	3 tablespoons mango chutney
salt and freshly ground black pepper	a little double cream (optional)
1 × 400g (14 oz) tin of sliced mango in syrup	some fresh coriander or flat-leaf parsley

1 Carefully remove the skin from the duck breasts. Preheat the ridged grill pan on the Boiling Plate. Rub the duck skin over the ridges to grease them.

2 Warm the toasted flaked almonds in the Simmering Oven on a plate.

3 Season the duck breasts with salt and pepper on each side. When the grill pan is hot, add the duck breasts and cook for about 5 minutes. Turn the breasts over and part cover with a lid. Cook for a further 5 minutes until the breasts are tender and pink in the middle. Remove the duck breasts from the grill pan and keep warm.

4 Pour the syrup from the can of mangoes into a pan, add the brandy and boil for a few minutes on the Boiling Plate, reducing until thick and syrupy. Slice the mango into pencil-thin strips and add to the brandy and syrup, with the mango chutney, lightly season and add cream (if using). Cook for only a moment.

5 Arrange the duck on a plate, sprinkle over the flaked almonds and serve with a little of the sauce. Serve the rest of the sauce separately. Garnish with coriander or flat-leaf parsley.

TO PREPARE AHEAD Skin the breasts and make the sauce up to 24 hours ahead. Add the mango at the last moment.

TO FREEZE Not suitable.

TO COOK IN A CONVENTIONAL OVEN Cook on the hob in the usual way.

WATERCROFT QUAIL

This is a variation on Watercroft Chicken (see page 74). Ask your good-quality independent butcher about boned quail. He can get them from his local speciality wholesalers or from Smithfield, Birmingham, Manchester, Glasgow and Edinburgh markets. If he has a problem, contact suppliers: The Teesdale Trencherman, Startforth Hall, Barnard Castle, Co. Durham DL12 9RA (Tel: 01833 638370), who also do mail order.

Serves 6–8

12 quail, boned
salt and freshly ground black pepper
2 tablespoons lime marmalade
25g (1 oz) butter

MUSHROOM FARCE
50g (2 oz) butter
3 shallots, finely chopped
350g (12 oz) button mushrooms,
 coarsely chopped
50g (2 oz) breadcrumbs (about 2 slices)
1 small egg, beaten

SAUCE
150ml (5 fl oz) good chicken stock
juice of 1 lime
1 × 200ml (7 fl oz) carton of
 crème fraîche
lots of chopped fresh parsley

1 For the mushroom farce, melt the butter in a pan on the Boiling Plate, and sauté the shallots for about 1 minute. Cover and transfer to the floor of the Simmering Oven for 10 minutes. Add the mushrooms, toss quickly in the butter, and cook for another 2 minutes on the Boiling Plate. Remove from the heat, add the breadcrumbs and egg, and season well. Leave to cool.

2 To stuff the quail, pull back the skin at the front of each bird, season and fill the cavity with the farce, using a dessertspoon, then fold back. Put all the quail into the large greased roasting tin.

3 Put the marmalade into a saucepan with the butter, and heat very gently on the Simmering Plate, stirring well, until the marmalade has melted and combined with the butter. Brush the birds with this mixture.

4 Cook in the Roasting Oven in the highest position for about 15 minutes until golden brown. Remove from the oven, transfer the birds to a warmed serving dish using a slotted spoon, and keep hot in the Simmering Oven while making the sauce.

5 To make the sauce, scrape all the bits from the base and sides of the roasting tin, add the stock and stir briskly to reduce a little on the floor of the Roasting Oven. Add the lime juice and crème fraîche and heat gently, stirring well, until it has a smooth creamy consistency. Season, add the chopped parsley and serve with the quail.

TO PREPARE AHEAD   Make the stuffing ahead of time and cool. Stuff the quail, cover and refrigerate for up to 24 hours.

TO FREEZE   Freeze the raw, stuffed quail for up to 3 months.

TO THAW   Defrost for about 4–6 hours at room temperature.

TO COOK IN A CONVENTIONAL OVEN   Cook the quail in the oven preheated to 200°C/400°F/Gas mark 6 for about 15–20 minutes until golden brown and tender.

BROWNING POULTRY AND MEAT

With short-term cooking – chicken, quail or rack of lamb, say – the Aga does not brown meats very well, so I glaze them with something like redcurrant jelly which gives the meat both colour and gloss. Here I use marmalade.

GUINEA FOWL WITH PORT AND BLUEBERRY SAUCE

For traditionalists like my husband, Paul, make the sauce in the recipe but don't add the blueberries!
If you joint the guinea fowl ahead you can use the carcass to make stock for the recipe.

Serves 8

2 guinea fowl, about 1kg (2¼ lb) each
salt and freshly ground black pepper
olive oil
fresh parsley (or thyme)

SAUCE
450ml (15 fl oz) guinea fowl or good
   chicken stock
3 tablespoons cornflour
100ml (4 fl oz) port
3 tablespoons redcurrant jelly
2 tablespoons soy sauce
1–2 tablespoons Worcestershire sauce
225g (8 oz) blueberries

1 Take off the thigh/leg joints and the breast/wing joints from the guinea fowl, making eight joints from the two birds. Trim off all excess fat and season well. (Make stock from the carcass and backbones: put bones in your smallest pan, cover with water and add vegetables to flavour.)

2 Fry the guinea fowl joints in a very little oil on both sides in a large non-stick frying pan on the Boiling Plate until golden. Remove from the pan and put to one side. Drain off any fat. Wipe out the frying pan.

3 Make the sauce by blending 4 tablespoons of stock with the cornflour in a bowl. Measure into the wiped frying pan the port, remaining stock, redcurrant jelly, soy sauce, Worcestershire sauce and some salt and pepper. Whisk in the blended cornflour mixture and bring to the boil on the Boiling Plate, allowing it to thicken.

4 Put the browned joints into the frying pan with the sauce. Bring to the boil, cover and transfer to the floor of the Simmering Oven, and cook for about 30 minutes or until tender.

5 In the last few minutes of cooking time, add the blueberries to the pan. Serve sprinkled with parsley (or thyme). Good with a mash (see page 136).

TO PREPARE AHEAD Cook completely without adding the blueberries, cool, and keep in the fridge for about 12 hours.

TO FREEZE As above. Cool, cover and freeze, for up to 1 month.

TO THAW   Thaw for about 6 hours at room temperature or overnight in the fridge.

TO REHEAT   Turn into a casserole. Reheat on the floor of the Roasting Oven for about 20 minutes, stirring from time to time. Add the blueberries when the guinea fowl is hot.

TO COOK IN A CONVENTIONAL OVEN   Cook in the oven preheated to 190°C/375°F/ Gas mark 5 for 20–30 minutes until tender.

ROAST PHEASANT WITH SCARLET CONFIT

For this recipe I roast the pheasants and serve only the breast meat. The next day I make a casserole of the legs (as for Loch Rannoch Venison, see page 98). The Scarlet Confit is a perfect accompaniment, see opposite.

Serves 4–6

	MARINADE
a brace of oven-ready pheasants	juice of 1 orange
150ml (5 fl oz) pheasant or chicken stock	2 tablespoons runny honey
1 teaspoon cornflour	2 tablespoons soy sauce
2 tablespoons port	1 tablespoon Worcestershire sauce
sprigs of fresh herbs	1 dessertspoon paprika

1 Take two large freezer bags and put one inside the other. Mix the orange juice, honey, soy sauce, Worcestershire sauce and paprika and put with the pheasants into the inner bag. Marinate for about 24 hours in the fridge.

2 Stand the pheasants skin side up on a sheet of foil in the small roasting tin. Reserve the marinade. Hang the tin on the top set of runners in the Roasting Oven and roast for 45 minutes, covering the breasts with foil when they are brown, after about 15 minutes. Lift the pheasants out and allow to rest in the Simmering Oven while you make the gravy.

3 Make the reserved marinade up to 300ml (10 fl oz) with the stock. Slake the cornflour with 2 tablespoons of marinade and stock, and pour back into the marinade with the port. Remove the foil from the roasting tin, tipping any juice back into the roasting tin, and pour in the marinade liquid. Return the roasting tin to the floor of the Roasting Oven for about 3–4 minutes, whisking a couple of times, until bubbling.

4 Carve each breast off the carcass and cut into about 5–7 slices. Arrange on each plate, garnish with a bouquet of fresh herbs and serve with the gravy and Scarlet Confit. Next day make a casserole with the legs (see above).

TO PREPARE AHEAD Marinate the pheasants for 24 hours ahead and make the gravy after this time.

TO FREEZE Not suitable.

TO COOK IN A CONVENTIONAL OVEN Roast at 220°C/425°F/Gas mark 7 for about 50 minutes, covering the breasts if getting too brown.

SCARLET CONFIT V

Gently reheat to serve with hot game casseroles and roast game birds. It's good with turkey too.

Serves 4–6

450g (1 lb) fresh or frozen cranberries	50ml (2 fl oz) cider vinegar
225g (8 oz) granulated sugar	a large pinch of ground allspice
zest and juice of 1 orange	a large pinch of ground cinnamon
50ml (2 fl oz) port	

1 Measure all the ingredients into a shallow stew pan, and bring to the boil on the Boiling Plate.

2 Place uncovered in the Simmering Oven for about 1 hour, stirring from time to time. Don't worry if it looks a bit runny as it thickens when it cools (so long as the cranberries are soft).

TO PREPARE AHEAD Make up to a month ahead and keep in the fridge.

TO COOK IN A CONVENTIONAL OVEN Cook on the hob in the usual way.

REMINDER

If you're worried that you might forget something in the Simmering Oven – with the Aga, there are no cooking smells to alert you! – simply tie a bright-coloured ribbon to the front rail. This will catch your eye and remind you. A timer is a must too.

CHASTLETON PHEASANT

Why Chastleton pheasant, you may ask? Well, it is Penny's invention, and she lives in Chastleton. Penny is at my side helping with Aga workshops, and she is an excellent cook, especially with game. Don't be tempted to overcook the breasts as they will be dry.

Serves 6

6 pheasant breasts, skinned
salt and freshly ground black pepper
8–12 slices Parma ham

STUFFING
a knob of butter
1 onion, finely chopped

3 cloves garlic, crushed
1 tablespoon sun-dried tomato paste

SAUCE
1 tablespoon sun-dried tomato paste
300ml (10 fl oz) double cream
a few basil leaves, freshly torn

1 For the stuffing, melt the butter in a pan and add the onion and garlic. Fry on the Boiling Plate for a few minutes, cover and transfer to the Simmering Oven for 15 minutes until the onion is tender. Stir in the sun-dried tomato paste, season with salt and pepper and cool.

2 Take the pheasant breasts and slit lengthways 1cm ($\frac{1}{2}$ in) down the breasts. Fill each with a sixth of the onion mixture. Season the breasts and wrap a piece of Parma ham round each one (1$\frac{1}{2}$ slices may be necessary depending on the size of the breasts).

3 Put the pheasant into the small roasting tin and roast on the top set of runners in the Roasting Oven for about 10 minutes until just done. Remove the pheasant breasts to a serving dish and keep warm.

4 Deglaze the pan with the sun-dried tomato paste and cream, season and put on the floor of the Roasting Oven for 4–5 minutes.

5 Slice the breasts into three diagonally and serve with a little of the sauce. Scatter over the torn basil leaves and serve.

TO PREPARE AHEAD Roast the pheasant breasts, put in a cold serving dish and pour over the sauce without the basil leaves. Cool, cover with foil and chill for 24 hours.

TO FREEZE Not suitable.

TO REHEAT Keep covered with foil and reheat in the Roasting Oven for about 10–15 minutes according to the thickness of the dish, until steaming and piping hot.

TO COOK IN A CONVENTIONAL OVEN Roast in the oven preheated to 200°C/400°F/ Gas mark 6 for about 15–20 minutes.

HIGHLAND PHEASANT WITH A TOUCH OF MANGO

This is an excellent recipe for using pheasants from the freezer when you are not too sure how long they've been there, or how old the birds are. It also produces plenty of delicious stock for use in other recipes.

Serves 6–8

a brace of pheasants	STOCK
salt and freshly ground black pepper	2 sticks celery
1 tablespoon vegetable oil	1 carrot
2 large onions, chopped	1 onion
50g (2 oz) plain flour	1 bay leaf
1 × 250ml (9 fl oz) carton of crème fraîche	a few parsley stalks
4 good tablespoons mango chutney	
3 tablespoons Worcestershire sauce	
1 small mango, chopped or sliced	
1 tablespoon chopped fresh parsley	

1 Make the stock the day before. Trim the skin and any excess fat from the pheasants and arrange snugly in a casserole or pan just large enough to take them with the stock ingredients and some seasoning. Cover with cold water, bring to the boil on the Boiling Plate, and simmer for 5 minutes. Cover and transfer to the Simmering Oven for 1½–2 hours until the pheasants are very tender. Leave to cool completely in the liquid. This will ensure that the pheasants are moist. Measure out 225ml (8 fl oz) stock to use in the dish.

2 When the pheasants are cool, carefully strip all the meat from the birds and cut into neat pieces, discarding all the bones and skin. Use the bones to enrich the leftover stock.

3 Heat the oil in a largish pan on the Boiling Plate, and sauté the onion for a few minutes. Cover and transfer to the Simmering Oven for about 15 minutes until soft.

4 Add the flour, then the measured stock, stirring well, to the onion on the Boiling Plate. When it boils, transfer to the Simmering Plate. Allow to thicken, then stir in the crème fraîche.

5 Stirring continually, add the mango chutney, Worcestershire sauce and some seasoning. Add half of the fresh mango and the strips of pheasant meat. If the sauce is a little thick, thin it down using more stock. Turn into an ovenproof dish (not too shallow).

6 Reheat the pheasant on the second set of runners in the Roasting Oven for about 15 minutes until brown on top and piping hot. Garnish with the remaining slices of fresh mango and the chopped parsley. Serve with mashed potato with added herbs and a good salad or broccoli.

TO PREPARE AHEAD   The recipe can be prepared ahead to the end of stage 5, but omitting the fresh mango. Cool, cover and refrigerate for up to 2 days.

TO FREEZE   Not suitable.

TO REHEAT   Stir in the fresh mango. Bring up to the boil on the Boiling Plate, then transfer to the Roasting Oven on the second set of runners and reheat for about 15 minutes, until piping hot.

TO COOK IN A CONVENTIONAL OVEN   Cook the pheasants in stage 1 on top of the hob, simmering gently for $1\frac{1}{2}$–2 hours until the pheasants are very tender. The exact time will depend upon the age of the pheasants. Complete the recipe, transferring the pheasant to the oven, preheated to 190°C/375°F/Gas mark 5 for about 20–30 minutes until piping hot and brown on top.

PERSONALISING RECIPES

When you make a successful change to a favourite recipe, pencil a note on the recipe itself or, if you don't like defacing your books, attach a little Post-it note. That way you won't make any mistakes the next time you use the recipe. I love a well-thumbed cookbook, even if it is a bit splattered!

LOCH RANNOCH VENISON

A wonderful rich winter casserole which is perfect for entertaining. Serve it with redcurrant or other fruit jelly, or serve simply with mashed potato for the family.

Serves 6–8

900g (2 lb) stewing venison, cut into 2.5cm (1 in) pieces

25g (1 oz) butter

100g (4 oz) smoked streaky bacon, snipped into small pieces

350g (12 oz) whole shallots or small pickling onions

2–3 cloves garlic, crushed

50g (2 oz) plain flour

300ml (10 fl oz) red wine

600ml (20 fl oz) chicken stock

1 tablespoon tomato purée

1 tablespoon runny honey

1 head of celery, cut diagonally (reserve the heart for later)

225g (8 oz) chestnut mushrooms, whole or, if large, halved

salt and freshly ground black pepper

celery leaves or fresh parsley

1 Brown the venison either by roasting in the Roasting Oven (see page 19) or brown in batches in a frying pan in butter on the Boiling Plate. Spoon into a large casserole.

2 Cook the bacon in the frying pan on the Boiling Plate until the fat begins to run. Add the whole shallots and garlic, and fry for about 4–5 minutes. Add the flour, stir well, then blend in the wine and stock. Add the tomato purée, honey, celery, whole mushrooms and the seasoning. Bring to the boil, and simmer for 5 minutes.

3 Pour the sauce over the venison in the casserole. Cover and transfer to the Simmering Oven for 1½–2½ hours, or until tender. Add the chopped heart of celery for the last 20 minutes of the cooking time. This adds crunch to the casserole.

4 Check the seasoning, skim off any fat and decorate with celery leaves or parsley.

TO PREPARE AHEAD After stage 3, quickly cool, cover and chill for 2 days.

TO FREEZE Cool, pack and freeze at the end of stage 3, for up to 3 months.

TO THAW Thaw overnight in the fridge.

TO REHEAT Bring up to the boil in an ovenproof casserole on the Boiling Plate, stir, then transfer to the Roasting Oven on the second set of runners and reheat for about 15 minutes, until piping hot.

TO COOK IN A CONVENTIONAL OVEN Cook at 160°C/325°F/Gas mark 3 for about 2 hours until the venison is tender.

PORK MIMOSA

The wonderful blend of spices gives a real mellowness to the sauce which is in no way hot and fiery. Serve with plain boiled rice and raita (see opposite), some mango chutney and a fresh mango, cut into cubes.

Creamed coconut comes in packets, and is usually found in good supermarkets near the curry powders in the Indian food section.

Serves 4

25g (1 oz) butter

900g (2 lb) pork fillet, cut in 1cm (½ in) slices

1 large Spanish onion, cut in wedges

2 fat cloves garlic, crushed

1 × 2.5cm (1 in) piece of fresh root ginger, peeled and finely chopped

1 level tablespoon each of ground cumin, ground coriander, ground turmeric and medium curry powder

salt and freshly ground black pepper

1 × 400g (14 oz) tin of chopped tomatoes

150ml (5 fl oz) chicken stock or water

50g (2 oz) creamed coconut, cut into pieces

1 × 250g (9 oz) carton of Greek yoghurt

fresh mint or coriander leaves

1 Melt the butter in a fairly large pan on the Boiling Plate and brown the meat. Lift out with a slotted spoon and put to one side.

2 Add the onion and garlic, turn, cover the pan and transfer to the floor of the Simmering Oven for 10 minutes.

3 Remove the lid, stand the pan on the Boiling Plate, and add the ginger and spices. Season and mix well. Stir in the tomatoes and stock, and bring to the boil, stirring. It will be a thick mixture at this stage. Drop in the meat and coconut, bring back to the boil and simmer for a few minutes.

4 Cover and transfer to the Simmering Oven for about 30 minutes, or until the meat is tender.

5 Before serving, stir in the yoghurt. Pour into a dish and decorate with the mint or coriander leaves. Serve with rice, raita, mango chutney and some fresh mango.

TO PREPARE AHEAD Can be made, cooled, covered and stored in the fridge for up to 3 days.

TO FREEZE Cool, then freeze at the end of stage 4 for up to 3 months.

TO THAW   Thaw for about 4 hours at room temperature, or overnight in the fridge.

TO REHEAT   Bring to the boil on the Boiling Plate, then transfer to the Roasting Oven on the second set of runners and reheat for about 15 minutes, until piping hot. Stir in the yoghurt.

TO COOK IN A CONVENTIONAL OVEN   Cook in the oven preheated to 160°C/325°F/ Gas mark 3, for about 1 hour or until the pork is tender. Stir in the yoghurt.

RAITA

A wonderful fresh accompaniment for any curry-flavoured casserole.

Serves 4

1 × 7.5cm (3 in) piece of cucumber, seeded and finely diced	1 × 150g (5 oz) carton of plain yoghurt
salt and freshly ground black pepper	about 6 sprigs of mint, chopped

1 Sprinkle the prepared cucumber with salt, leave for half an hour, then drain off the liquid. Mix with the yoghurt and the freshly chopped mint. Season with pepper and spoon into a serving bowl.

RICE

A faultless way of oven cooking rice, using the absorption method. Be exact with quantities and every grain of rice will be separate.

Serves 4

275g (10 oz) par-boiled or easy-cook rice (Uncle Ben's)	50g (2 oz) wild rice
	salt

1 Measure the easy-cook rice and the wild rice into a pan, add 450ml (15 fl oz) water and 1 teaspoon salt. Bring to the boil, cover, and place on the floor of the Simmering Oven for about 15–20 minutes until the liquid is absorbed and the rice is tender.

MARINATED PORK WITH PINEAPPLE AND THYME

If buying from your butcher, ask for boned loin. In supermarkets it is sometimes called 'traditional loin steak'. It is very lean, and comes well trimmed. You will have to ask for it at the meat counter.

Serves 6–8

1.4kg (3 lb) boned loin of pork, from the thin end nearest the leg, skin removed	MARINADE 250ml (8 fl oz) pineapple juice from a carton 2 tablespoons maple syrup (or use honey) 3 tablespoons soy sauce 2 cloves garlic, crushed a handful of fresh thyme, or 2 heaped teaspoons dried thyme 1 teaspoon ground coriander

1 Make up the marinade by mixing everything together. Take two large freezer bags and put one inside the other. Put the pork and the marinade into the inner bag, tie up and leave for at least 12 hours in the fridge, turning occasionally.

2 Remove the pork from the marinade and reserve the liquid. Lie the pork flat in the small roasting tin, skin side uppermost. Cover loosely with a piece of foil.

3 Hang the roasting tin on the third set of runners in the Roasting Oven, and roast for 50 minutes. Remove the foil, pour over the marinade and roast for a further 20–30 minutes until the marinade has darkened and the pork is cooked. If getting too brown, replace the foil. Test to see if it is cooked by spearing the centre with a skewer: if the juices that flow are clear it is done; if pink, leave a little longer.

4 Rest the pork for 10 minutes before carving. Serve with the strained marinade gravy. If liked, it may be thickened.

TO PREPARE AHEAD Marinate the pork for at least 12 hours ahead.

TO FREEZE Freeze raw, in the marinade, in a plastic bag for up to 2 months.

TO THAW Thaw for at least 8 hours at room temperature, or overnight in the fridge.

TO COOK IN A CONVENTIONAL OVEN Cook in the oven preheated to 200°C/400°F/ Gas mark 6, for about $1\frac{1}{2}$ hours.

CUMBERLAND CRUSTED LAMB

A perfect chance to use up the last of the Christmas walnuts that have sat around in the fruit bowl. This recipe is easy to prepare, with an equally quick and simple sauce.

Serves 6

2 lean racks of lamb, the chop bones cut short, chine removed

½ egg, beaten

2 fat cloves garlic, quartered

a generous bunch of fresh parsley, about 25g (1 oz), washed

1 slice of wholemeal bread

2 tablespoons shelled walnut pieces

grated rind of 1 small lemon

1 tablespoon walnut oil, if you have some

salt and freshly ground black pepper

SAUCE

1 heaped teaspoon plain flour

juice of ½ lemon

juice and zest of 1 orange

300ml (10 fl oz) red wine

about 3 good tablespoons redcurrant jelly

1 Trim any surplus fat from the lamb. Paint the outside fat surface of the two lamb racks with a little beaten egg and reserve the rest for the crust.

2 Using the metal blade of the processor, process the garlic briefly then add the parsley and briefly process again. Add the slice of bread and process to the count of 10. Add the walnuts, lemon rind and walnut oil and process to the count of 15. Add salt, pepper and remaining egg, and whizz to combine.

3 Divide the crust mixture in half and spread on the outside of each rack of lamb. Prepare this ahead and chill for half an hour if time allows as this helps to hold the crust.

4 Place the racks in the small roasting tin in the Roasting Oven, bone ends towards the centre, for 25 minutes on the second set of runners – or, for very pink, 20 minutes.

5 When the lamb is cooked, put it on a serving dish to keep warm while making the sauce.

6 For the sauce, on the Simmering Plate add the flour to the roasting tin juices and scrape up all the bits, using a whisk if necessary. Add the lemon and orange juices, red wine, orange zest and redcurrant jelly, and whisk again. Slide the tin on to the floor of the Roasting Oven and cook for 5 minutes, whisking once. Taste for seasoning, and sieve.

TO PREPARE AHEAD Prepare the lamb up to the end of stage 3 up to 12 hours ahead.

TO FREEZE Not suitable.

TO COOK IN A CONVENTIONAL OVEN Roast at 220°C/425°F/Gas mark 7 for about 15 minutes for rare, 20 minutes for well done.

GLAZED LOIN OF LAMB WITH SAUCE PALOISE

A very special and modern, French cut of lamb, fillet of loin is the eye meat of loin chops. The paloise sauce can be made ahead, but cannot be reheated because it would split. It can be kept warm, covered, on the back of the Aga, or you can serve it lukewarm. If liked, make proper gravy, see page 106.

Serves 4

2 lamb loins, defatted and boneless,
  about 450g (1 lb) total weight
1–2 tablespoons redcurrant jelly
salt and freshly ground black pepper

PALOISE SAUCE
1 quantity Hollandaise Sauce
  (see opposite)
1 teaspoon mint sauce concentrate
1 teaspoon chopped fresh mint

1 Line the small roasting tin with foil. Spread the lamb fillets with the redcurrant jelly, season well and sit the lamb on the foil in the roasting tin.

2 Roast at the top of the Roasting Oven for 10–15 minutes. Turn once during this time to achieve an even glaze. Allow the meat to rest for 5–10 minutes.

3 Meanwhile make the paloise sauce by simply mixing the hollandaise sauce, mint sauce and fresh mint. Keep warm on the back of the Aga on a folded tea-towel.

4 Carve the lamb into 1cm (½ in) diagonal slices and serve with the paloise sauce.

TO PREPARE AHEAD Have the lamb ready in the roasting tin spread with jelly as in stage 1 a few hours ahead. The sauce can be made an hour in advance.

TO FREEZE Not suitable.

TO COOK IN A CONVENTIONAL OVEN Quickly brown the meat on both sides in a non-stick frying pan, spread with redcurrant jelly, then cook at 220°C/425°F/Gas mark 7 for about 10–15 minutes.

HOLLANDAISE SAUCE

If you have a large processor it is a good idea to tilt the machine so that the mixture gathers on one side. No need to tilt it in a blender or small processor. If you have no unsalted butter, use salted and discard the last runny, watery bit in the pan at the end.

Hollandaise can be varied in a number of ways, see below and opposite. Needless to say, any herbs must be fresh or frozen and not dried.

Makes 300ml (10 fl oz)

6 tablespoons white wine vinegar	225g (8 oz) unsalted butter
6 black peppercorns	salt and freshly ground black pepper
½ bay leaf	4 egg yolks

1 Put the vinegar, peppercorns and bay leaf into a small pan and reduce on the Boiling Plate to about 1 tablespoon.

2 Melt the butter until boiling in another small pan on the same plate.

3 Thoroughly preheat the processor blade and bowl by pouring boiling water in, and then discarding the water.

4 Pour the egg yolks into the hot processor with the machine running. Strain in the warm vinegar and, still with the machine running, slowly trickle in the boiling, melted butter by pouring through the funnel. When all the butter has been added, season carefully. It should be lightly piquant, barely holding its shape, and lukewarm rather than hot.

BÉARNAISE SAUCE For fish or meat. Add 1 tablespoon each chopped fresh thyme, parsley and marjoram.

TARRAGON OR DILL SAUCE For fish. Add 2 tablespoons chopped fresh dill or 1 tablespoon chopped fresh tarragon.

CHIVE SAUCE For meat, fish or eggs. Add 2 tablespoons chopped fresh chives.

MUSTARD OR HORSERADISH SAUCE For beef. Add 2 tablespoons Dijon mustard or 2 tablespoons strong horseradish.

TO PREPARE AHEAD Make an hour ahead and keep warm on the back of the Aga, standing on a tea-towel in the serving dish, or transfer to a heated wide-necked thermos flask to keep warm for up to 4 hours.

TO FREEZE Not suitable.

FRENCH-STYLE RACK OF LAMB
WITH PROPER GRAVY

Rack of lamb is a roast for a special occasion. You may need to order it from your butcher in advance. To colour and glaze the meat, use some redcurrant jelly – which also adds flavour.

Serves 4–6

2 fully trimmed French-style racks of
    lamb, chine bone removed (usually 14
    cutlets in total, 7 in each rack)
olive oil
salt and freshly ground black pepper
1 tablespoon redcurrant jelly

GRAVY
1 level tablespoon plain flour
65ml (2½ fl oz) red wine
300ml (10 fl oz) chicken stock
1 teaspoon Worcestershire sauce
1 teaspoon lemon juice
1 tablespoon redcurrant jelly
a dash of gravy browning

1 Rub the lamb with a little olive oil. Season well and spread with the redcurrant jelly.

2 Sit the lamb in the small roasting tin, the bone tips facing downwards and inwards. Roast at the top of the Roasting Oven for 12–15 minutes for pink lamb, 20 minutes for well done. This will depend on the thickness of the rack of lamb.

3 Wrap loosely in foil, and transfer to the Simmering Oven while you make the gravy.

4 Off the heat, blend in the flour with the fat and juices in the tin, using a metal whisk. Pour in the wine and remaining ingredients, whisk well, then slide on to the floor of the Roasting Oven for about 5 minutes until bubbling and slightly thickened. Check the seasoning.

5 Serve two to three cutlets per person with the gravy, and perhaps potato cakes (see page 134), stir-fried young spinach and young carrots.

TO PREPARE AHEAD The lamb can be spread with redcurrant jelly a few hours ahead. The red wine, Worcestershire sauce, lemon juice and redcurrant jelly can all be added to the stock ready to make the gravy.

TO FREEZE Not suitable.

TO COOK IN A CONVENTIONAL OVEN Roast at 220°C/425°F/Gas mark 7 for about 15 minutes for rare, 20 minutes for well done.

GLORIOUS LAMB WITH RED ONIONS AND PEPPERS

You could use thick slices from a leg of lamb or, indeed, half a leg of lamb taken from the knuckle end. Knuckles are usually taken from the shoulder of lamb, and are often available frozen.

Serves 6

6 knuckles of lamb	150ml (5 fl oz) red wine
4 fat cloves garlic, roughly chopped	3 tablespoons redcurrant jelly
2 large red peppers, seeded and roughly sliced	salt and freshly ground black pepper
3 red onions, quartered	a little dried rosemary
1 × 225g (8 oz) tin of chopped tomatoes	2 tablespoons chopped fresh parsley

1 Arrange the knuckles in the greased large roasting tin, and slide on to the top set of runners in the Roasting Oven. Brown the joints, turning once. This will take about 30 minutes or so.

2 Lift out the knuckles, drain off any fat and transfer to a deep casserole dish, large enough to take the knuckles plus vegetables. Add the garlic, peppers, onions, tomatoes and their liquid, wine, redcurrant jelly, salt, pepper and rosemary. Arrange the knuckles on top, season them, then bring to the boil on the Boiling Plate and cover with a lid or foil.

3 Transfer to the Simmering Oven for about 3 hours or until the meat is exceedingly tender and falling off the bone. Check the seasoning of the juices. If there is any fat on the surface, blot off with kitchen paper.

4 Sprinkle parsley over each knuckle when serving with the vegetables and juices. Serve with creamy mashed potatoes.

TO PREPARE AHEAD All the vegetables can be prepared the day before.

TO FREEZE Not suitable.

TO COOK IN A CONVENTIONAL OVEN Cook in the oven preheated to 160°C/325°F/ Gas mark 3 for about 2–2½ hours until tender.

KLEFTIKO

This Greek dish is very easy, cooked for ages in the Simmering Oven until the meat falls off the bone. Use six knuckles of lamb instead of shoulder if preferred. The juices are thin for this recipe, so if a thicker sauce is preferred, thicken with a little cornflour and keep the lamb warm whilst this is being done.

Serves 6

1.4–1.8kg (3–4 lb) lean shoulder of lamb, boned	juice of 1 lemon
4 fat cloves garlic, cut in spikes	1 tablespoon fresh rosemary
2 large mild onions, sliced	1 tablespoon fresh marjoram
salt and freshly ground black pepper	chopped fresh parsley

1 Open out the shoulder of lamb flat and remove any pockets of fat and excess fat. Make incisions into the lamb with a sharp pointed knife and in each hole slip a spike of garlic. Lie the lamb flat in the roasting tin, skin side down.

2 Slide the tin on to the top set of runners in the Roasting Oven and brown the meat. It will take about 30 minutes.

3 Lift out, remove any fat from the roasting tin, add the onions to the tin, season and add lemon juice and herbs. Return the lamb to the tin, skin side up. Return to the Roasting Oven on the top set of runners and brown. It will take 20 minutes or so.

4 Transfer to a large ovenproof casserole, cover and bring to the boil, then transfer to the Simmering Oven for 1½–2 hours until really tender.

5 Carve, and serve with the onions and juices and a sprinkling of parsley.

TO PREPARE AHEAD   Complete stage 1 and prepare the vegetables the day before.

TO FREEZE   Not suitable.

TO COOK IN A CONVENTIONAL OVEN   Brown the meat first in a non-stick frying pan then cook slowly in the oven at 160°C/325°F/Gas mark 3 with the other ingredients for about 2 hours or until tender.

FILLET STEAK WITH WILD MUSHROOM SAUCE

If one could give marks for a recipe, this would get 10 out of 10! It's a foolproof way of cooking fillet steaks ahead. Serve with a delicious mushroom sauce which can also be made ahead.

Serves 4

4 x 175g (6 oz) thick fillet steaks	SAUCE
olive oil	25g (1 oz) butter
salt and freshly ground black pepper	1 clove garlic, crushed
a little butter	2 level tablespoons plain flour
chopped fresh parsley	scant 65ml (2½ fl oz) Madeira
	1 x 295g (11 oz) tin of Campbell's concentrated beef consommé
	175g (6 oz) mixed wild mushrooms (chestnut, oyster and shiitake), sliced
	2 generous tablespoons crème fraîche
	1 tablespoon chopped fresh parsley

1 Oil the steaks lightly on both sides, and season well.

2 Preheat the grill pan first on the Simmering Plate, then on the Boiling Plate until very hot.

3 Sear the steaks for 2 minutes each side for medium rare, a little longer if you like the steaks well done. Place on Lift-Off paper on a baking sheet. When cold, place in the fridge covered with clingfilm. (Or, of course, you can carry straight on!)

4 To make the sauce, melt the butter on the Simmering Plate, and add the garlic. Blend in the flour, off the heat, followed by the Madeira and consommé. Add the sliced mushrooms. Return to the Simmering Plate, and bring to the boil, stirring until thickened. Add the crème fraîche and parsley, and check the seasoning.

5 Bring the steaks to room temperature for 30 minutes, then uncover. Still on the Lift-Off paper, smear the smallest amount of butter on top of each steak, then place on the grid shelf in the centre of the Roasting Oven for 7 minutes. Don't be tempted to leave it longer, otherwise the steaks will be over-cooked. Reheat very thin steaks for 6 minutes.

6 Reheat the sauce in a pan on the Simmering Plate.

7 Serve the steaks immediately with a tablespoon of mushroom sauce alongside. Sprinkle with freshly chopped parsley and serve the rest of the sauce separately.

TO PREPARE AHEAD   For the steaks, complete stages 1, 2 and 3, up to 12 hours ahead. The sauce can be made the day before and kept in the fridge.

TO FREEZE   Not suitable.

TO COOK IN A CONVENTIONAL OVEN   Cook the steaks and the sauce on the hob.

BURLINGTON BEEF

A tasty beef casserole, good enough for a supper party. The stir-fried garnish gives a lovely crunch to the dish. Serve with creamy mashed potato.

Serves 6

25g (1oz) dried mushrooms
    (I use shiitake)
450ml (15 fl oz) beef stock, hot
2 tablespoons sunflower oil
1kg (2¼ lb) good-quality braising steak,
    diced
2 tablespoons plain flour
150ml (5 fl oz) dry white wine
350g (12 oz) onions, thinly sliced
4 sticks celery, strings removed and
    diagonally sliced
4 cloves garlic, crushed
2 tablespoons apricot jam
a sprig of fresh thyme

salt and freshly ground black pepper
¾ yellow pepper, seeded and thinly
    sliced
1 tablespoon balsamic vinegar
2 tablespoons chopped fresh flat-leaf
    parsley

GARNISH
1 tablespoon olive oil
¼ yellow pepper, seeded and cut into
    julienne strips
175g (6 oz) chestnut mushrooms, thinly
    sliced
6 sprigs fresh flat-leaf parsley

1 Wash the dried mushrooms and soak in hot stock for 20-30 minutes.

2 Heat the oil in a large pan on the Boiling Plate and brown the beef in batches, then remove from the pan. Slide the pan on to the Simmering Plate and blend in the flour. Blend in the white wine, dried mushrooms and soaking liquid. Add the onion, celery and garlic and cook for 5-6 minutes, stirring from time to time. Return the meat to the pan, bring to the boil and simmer for a few minutes. Stir in the apricot jam, sprig of thyme and season. Cover the pan and transfer to the floor of the Simmering Oven. Cook until tender, approximately 2½ hours.

3 About 20 minutes before the end of the cooking time, add the yellow pepper.

4 When nearly ready to serve, stir-fry in the olive oil the garnish vegetables.

5 Add the balsamic vinegar and chopped parsley to the stew and spoon on to warmed plates. Top with a heaped spoonful of the garnish vegetables and a sprig of parsley.

TO PREPARE AHEAD Make the dish to the end of stages 4 and add balsamic vinegar. Stir-fry the garnish vegetables and serve.

TO FREEZE Freeze the cold casserole, at the end of stage 4, for up to 3 months.

TO THAW   Thaw overnight in the fridge.

TO REHEAT   Bring up to the boil in an ovenproof casserole on the Boiling Plate, stir, then transfer to the Roasting Oven on the second set of runners and reheat for about 20 minutes. Stir-fry the garnish vegetables, complete stage 6 and serve.

TO COOK IN A CONVENTIONAL OVEN   Cook in the oven, preheated to 160°C/325°F/ Gas mark 3 for about 2 hours, then add the yellow pepper. Complete stages 4 and 6.

THAI BURGERS

This is a wonderful new way to do burgers – great for a different summer barbecue – but don't over-cook them.

Serves 6

450g (1 lb) best minced steak	½ teaspoon freshly ground black pepper
3–4 spring onions, thinly sliced	olive or sunflower oil
1 teaspoon ground coriander	1 large bunch of fresh coriander
3 teaspoons red Thai curry paste	crème fraîche
½ teaspoon salt	

1 Mix the steak, spring onions, coriander, curry paste, salt and pepper together in a large bowl, using your hands, making sure all the spices are evenly distributed.

2 Wet your hands and shape the mixture into six even-sized flat cakes.

3 Preheat a ridged grill pan until very hot on the Boiling Plate. Brush both sides of the burgers with olive or sunflower oil and fry for 2½–3½ minutes each side. Lift out of the pan as soon as they are cooked (if they stay in the pan they will over-cook). They are best just pink in the middle.

4 Serve the burgers on a bed of fresh coriander leaves with some crème fraîche to accompany. You can also serve 5cm (2 in) strips of spring onions fried on the grill pan.

TO PREPARE AHEAD   Complete stage 2. Cover and chill for up to 12 hours.

TO FREEZE   Wrap and freeze at the end of stage 2 for up to 1 month.

TO THAW   Thaw for about 4 hours at room temperature.

TO COOK IN A CONVENTIONAL OVEN   Simply cook on the hob in the usual way.

WARM FILLET OF BEEF SALAD

This is a wonderfully delicious, quick salad, ideal for a lunch or light supper. If you prefer, serve it on a green salad or warm roasted vegetables, rather than celery and cucumber.

Serves 4

4 fillet steaks	MARINADE
6 spring onions	2 tablespoons soy sauce
I small head of celery	2 tablespoons Worcestershire sauce
½–¾ cucumber	2 tablespoons soft brown sugar
olive oil	2 level teaspoons tomato purée
	I tablespoon white wine vinegar
	I tablespoon sesame seeds
	2 tablespoons olive oil
	2 cloves garlic, crushed
	I × 2.5cm (I in) piece of fresh root ginger, peeled and grated
	salt and freshly ground black pepper

1 Measure the marinade ingredients into a large bowl and mix together.

2 Cut the steaks into neat 5cm × 5mm (2 × ¼ in) strips and marinate in the bowl for at least 3 hours – overnight for best results.

3 Thinly slice the spring onions and celery on the diagonal. Cut the cucumber lengthways, take seeds out with a teaspoon or melon scoop, and slice thinly in horseshoe-shaped slices. Leave in a polythene bag in the fridge until required.

4 Heat a little oil in a large non-stick frying pan on the Boiling Plate. Drain the meat from the marinade (keep this), and quickly fry in two batches in the hot pan to seal and brown the meat. Drain from the pan and keep warm.

5 Add the reserved marinade to the pan and boil up on the Boiling Plate until syrupy. Return all the meat to the pan and stir until boiling. Pile the chilled, seasoned vegetables on a serving plate and pour over the beef with the sauce. Serve at once.

TO PREPARE AHEAD   A day ahead, make the vegetable salad and keep in the fridge in a polythene bag. Marinate the beef in the fridge overnight.

TO FREEZE   Not suitable.

TO COOK IN A CONVENTIONAL OVEN   Cook on the hob in the usual way.

OLD-FASHIONED PRESSED TONGUE

One in five people hate tongue; therefore it is only suitable for a mixed buffet. The rest love it, but I still buy a smaller tongue if I can. My family butcher always stocks it, but few do, and supermarkets do not always have it. Most butchers will put one in salt brine for you, but it takes time. Ask the butcher if the tongue needs soaking before cooking.

Serves 10–12, depending on size

1 salted ox tongue	1 bay leaf
1 onion	½ packet of powdered gelatine

1 Trim off any bits of fat from the tongue. Put in a pan of cold water with the onion and bay leaf and bring to the boil on the Boiling Plate. Simmer for 5 minutes, then transfer to the Simmering Oven for about 5 hours until tender. You might like to test the liquid at the end of 2 hours. If it is very salty, change the liquid and add fresh water. (I don't, my butcher does it just right.)

2 Take the tongue out of the pan and put it on a board. You might like to put on rubber gloves, it is jolly hot! Skin it and take off any fat (there might even be a little bone), then cut it in half horizontally. Choosing a container for the tongue is difficult: it should be small and high. My favourite pan is round, 9cm (3½ in) high and 14cm (5½ in) wide. A smallish round cake tin might serve as a mould.

3 Next make the jelly, using the cooking liquid. Put the gelatine in a teacup with 3 tablespoons cold water. Stand the cup in a pan of water on the Simmering Plate and heat until dissolved. Add 150ml (5 fl oz) of the liquid from the tongue.

4 Curl the cut halves of the tongue round in the container. Pour on the dissolved liquid and press down with a saucer or small plate with as heavy a weight on top as possible. Put into the fridge to set overnight.

5 The tongue is quite tricky to turn out. Gently heat the pan just enough to melt the jelly slightly to free it from the pan. If you heat the pan too much the jelly will run, so go carefully. The best way of heating is to run exceedingly hot water over the base of the pan or tin. Turn out on to a platter, and slice.

TO PREPARE AHEAD   Complete stage 4. It will store in the fridge for 4 days.

TO FREEZE   Not suitable.

TO COOK IN A CONVENTIONAL OVEN   Cook on the hob very slowly.

MEGA ROASTED VEGETABLE CIABATTA V

This is a wonderful dish for lunch or to eat outside. The secret of its success is to weight it down in the fridge, otherwise the filling is prone to fall out. It can be eaten cold but I'd rather not! I really suggest you serve it warm. It is crunchy too. Use coarsely grated Gruyère instead of Brie if you prefer.

Serves 4–6

1 small aubergine
salt and freshly ground black pepper
olive oil
100g (4 oz) chestnut mushrooms,
    coarsely sliced
½ head of fennel, thinly sliced
½ onion, thinly sliced
1 ciabatta loaf, cut in half horizontally
2 tablespoons red or green pesto
3 sun-dried tomatoes in oil, finely
    snipped
100g (4 oz) Brie, thinly sliced

DRESSING
2 tablespoons olive oil
1 teaspoon balsamic vinegar
1 teaspoon caster sugar
1 teaspoon red or green pesto
freshly torn basil leaves

1 Slice the aubergine into thin slices lengthways. Sprinkle with salt and pepper. Toss in a little oil and turn into the large roasting tin. Put on the floor of the Roasting Oven for about 2 minutes on each side. Remove and drain the aubergines on kitchen paper.

2 Add the mushrooms, fennel and onion together to the roasting tin and return to the floor of the Roasting Oven for a further 5 minutes.

3 Remove a little of the soft dough from the ciabatta and spread each inside with a tablespoon of pesto.

4 Mix together all the ingredients for the dressing, seasoning with salt and pepper, and sprinkle a little over the base half of the loaf.

5 Layer the aubergine, mushroom, fennel and onion, snipped sun-dried tomato and slices of Brie on the base half of the ciabatta, sprinkling seasoning and dressing between the layers until all the dressing and vegetables are used. Put the top half on to the loaf and press down firmly. Wrap very tightly in clingfilm and with foil. Weight down in the fridge for a minimum of 40 minutes. Remove clingfilm and foil.

6 Reheat in the roasting tin on the second set of runners in the Roasting Oven for about 10 minutes until crisp and warm right through. Serve in slices with a green salad.

TO PREPARE AHEAD   The whole loaf may be assembled to the end of stage 5 and kept in the fridge for up to 24 hours.

TO FREEZE   Not suitable.

TO COOK IN A CONVENTIONAL OVEN   Char-grill the vegetables at 220°C/425°F/ Gas mark 7 for about 20 minutes. Bake the loaf at the same temperature for about 10 minutes.

USE YOUR LOAF

Never throw away any dough that you remove from the ciabatta here, or any other bread. Freeze it, then use in stuffings and bread sauce – or dry (good in the Warming Oven of a four-oven Aga or Simmering Oven for a shorter time) to use as a breadcrumb coating.

GARLIC CHEESE AND
ROAST VEGETABLE NAAN BREAD V

A wonderful light supper or lunch dish served with green salad. You could also use this topping on pitta bread or on bruschetta.

Makes 4

1 red pepper	1 × 80g (3 oz) Boursin cheese with
1 yellow pepper	garlic and herbs
1 aubergine, sliced	4 mini naan breads
1 medium onion, peeled and sliced	a few drops of balsamic vinegar
2 tablespoons olive oil	chopped fresh parsley
salt and freshly ground black pepper	

1 Quarter the peppers lengthways, remove the seeds, and cut the flesh into chunky pieces.

2 Mix all the vegetables together in the large roasting tin with the olive oil and season with salt and pepper. Roast the vegetables for 20–25 minutes on the floor of the Roasting Oven, turning over half way through the cooking time, or until charred. Or you can grill the vegetables in two batches on the hot grill pan on the Boiling Plate.

3 Spread a quarter of the garlic and herb cheese over each naan bread. Divide the lightly charred vegetables over the cheese bases. Transfer to a large roasting tin, greased or lined with Lift-Off paper.

4 Bake for approximately 10 minutes on the second set of runners in the Roasting Oven until hot right through and crisp. Drizzle with a few drops of balsamic vinegar and chopped parsley and serve immediately.

TO PREPARE AHEAD Prepare to the end of stage 3, up to 12 hours in advance.

TO FREEZE Not suitable.

TO COOK IN A CONVENTIONAL OVEN Cook in the oven preheated to 220°C/425°F/Gas mark 7 for about 10–15 minutes.

MY PISSALADIÈRE V

This is a speciality of Provence, and is the French equivalent of the Italian pizza. The traditional recipe has a yeast dough base (like a pizza), and the topping includes anchovies and omits cheese. My version is a cross between the two!

Serves 6

	TOPPING
50g (2 oz) poppy seeds	3 tablespoons olive oil
175g (6 oz) plain flour	2 large onions, roughly chopped
90g (3½ oz) butter	3 fat cloves garlic, crushed
1 tablespoon light muscovado sugar	1 × 400g (14 oz) tin of chopped
salt and freshly ground black pepper	tomatoes
about 1–2 tablespoons water	1 × 140g (5 oz) tin of tomato purée
	2 teaspoons dried basil
	1 teaspoon caster sugar
	100g (4 oz) Vignotte cheese, coarsely
	grated
	75g (3 oz) pitted black olives
	freshly chopped basil or parsley

1 To make the poppy seed base, put the poppy seeds, flour, butter, sugar, salt and pepper into the processor. Process until it resembles fine breadcrumbs, then add the water. Process until just beginning to gather together into a ball, adding a shade more liquid if necessary.

2 Roll out straight on to Lift-Off paper on a flat baking tray, 28 × 38cm (11 × 15 in), into a circle about 30cm (12 in) in diameter. Pinch up the edge all round. The pastry is quite crumbly but patches up easily, and you can help to make the circle using your hands as well as a rolling pin. Rest in the fridge while making the filling.

3 Measure the oil into a saucepan, add the onions and garlic, and fry on the Boiling Plate for 2–3 minutes, stirring all the time. Cover and transfer to the floor of the Simmering Oven for about 20 minutes.

4 Remove the pan from the oven, add the chopped tomatoes, tomato purée, basil, sugar, and some salt and pepper, and bring to the boil on the Boiling Plate. Continue to boil rapidly, uncovered, until it is a thick consistency, about 5–7 minutes.

5 Fill the poppy seed pastry base with the tomato mixture, and sprinkle with the Vignotte cheese. Press the olives over the top.

6 Bake on the floor of the Roasting Oven for about 25–30 minutes. Check after 20 minutes that the pastry edge is not burning. If it is, slide the cold shelf into the oven on the second set of runners for the last 10 minutes or so. Scatter with chopped fresh basil or parsley, and serve hot.

TO PREPARE AHEAD Prepare the poppy seed base 24 hours ahead of time, roll out on to the baking sheet, cover and keep in the fridge. Prepare the filling for the pissaladière 48 hours in advance, cool, cover and keep in the fridge.

TO FREEZE Wrap the cooked pissaladière, once thoroughly cooled, very thoroughly, and freeze for up to 2 months.

TO THAW Thaw overnight in the fridge or at room temperature for about 6 hours.

TO REHEAT Slip on to a flat baking sheet and reheat on the floor of the Roasting Oven for about 10–15 minutes.

TO COOK IN A CONVENTIONAL OVEN Cook the tomato filling on the hob in the usual way. Bake the poppy seed base in the oven preheated to 220°C/425°F/Gas mark 7, for 15 minutes, then fill with the tomato mixture, cheese and olives. Bake for a further 15–20 minutes.

Any other rich, soft, flavoursome cheese can be used instead of Vignotte, e.g. Port Salut or blue cheese, or indeed a mixture left over from the cheese board. Decorate with anchovy fillets as well as olives if your family likes them: use one 50g (2 oz) tin of anchovy fillets, and divide each fillet lengthways.

TAGLIATELLE ST JACQUES

This delicious pasta dish brings back wonderful memories of eating outside in southern Italy.

Serves 4

275g (10 oz) dried tagliatelle	150ml (5 fl oz) double cream
salt and freshly ground black pepper	100g (4 oz) squid, cut into strips or rings
2 tablespoons good olive oil	4 large scallops with coral
1 large onion, finely chopped	100g (4 oz) button mushrooms, sliced
1 fat clove garlic, crushed	100g (4 oz) peeled prawns
100ml (4 fl oz) white wine	4 tablespoons chopped fresh parsley

1 Add the pasta to a large pan of boiling salted water. Bring to the boil on the Boiling Plate, then cover and cook on the Simmering Plate for 12 minutes until al dente. Drain and set to one side.

2 Heat the oil in a pan on the Boiling Plate and cook the onion and garlic for about 2 minutes, then stir in the wine and boil to reduce to about 2 tablespoons. Add the cream and boil to reduce to a thick sauce.

3 Add the squid to the sauce and cook for 1 minute on the Boiling Plate, then add the scallops and mushrooms and cook for a further 2 minutes, stirring well.

4 Lastly add the prawns and chopped parsley (saving a little to sprinkle over the finished dish). Bring to the boil on the Boiling Plate, and stir in the pasta and seasoning. Serve immediately in individual bowls or plates, with spoons so that none of the sauce is wasted.

TO PREPARE AHEAD Chop and slice the ingredients ahead of time on the day. The dish is then very quick to make.

TO FREEZE Not suitable.

TO COOK IN A CONVENTIONAL OVEN Cook on the hob in the usual way.

PENNE ITALIANO ^V

This wonderful pasta dish was invented by Lucy Young who runs our Aga workshops. It is best using fresh young spinach, which you mix in at the end of cooking. No extra salt is needed as Stilton is a salty cheese.

Serves 4–6

350g (12 oz) dried penne (quills)	300ml (10 fl oz) double cream
salt and freshly ground black pepper	juice of ½ lemon
a good knob of butter	75g (3 oz) fresh spinach, washed,
2 large cloves garlic, crushed	trimmed and shredded
225g (8 oz) small chestnut	75g (3 oz) blue Stilton cheese, grated
mushrooms, sliced	a good grating of nutmeg

1 Add the pasta to a large pan of boiling salted water. Bring to the boil on the Boiling Plate, then cover and cook on the Simmering Plate for 12 minutes, until al dente. Drain and set to one side.

2 Melt the butter in a large, deep, non-stick frying pan on the Boiling Plate, add the garlic and cook for a few moments. Add the mushrooms and allow to cook on the Simmering Plate for a couple of minutes. Stir in the cream and allow to boil until coating consistency.

3 Add the cooked pasta to the mushrooms and cream and stir well. Mix in the lemon juice, spinach and Stilton, and season with nutmeg and pepper. Stir well. Serve with a tossed green salad.

TO PREPARE AHEAD   All the ingredients can be prepared ahead, then it just takes 10 minutes to cook the pasta, during which time the sauce is made.

TO FREEZE   Not suitable

TO COOK IN A CONVENTIONAL OVEN   Cook on the hob in the usual way.

Serve some Black Olive and Cheese Bread
(see page 198) with your penne.

PASTA MILANO

This pasta dish, made with fusilli, is inexpensive and a real winner for flavour. I never use just pork sausagemeat, as I find it far too fatty. I buy good pork sausages, preferably the true Luganega Italian sausages. Waitrose Gourmet sausages do well.

Take care when chopping the chilli: wash your hands straight afterwards and do not put your hands near your eyes. If in doubt, chop with a knife and fork or wearing rubber gloves.

Serves 4

350g (12 oz) dried fusilli (corkscrew or spiral shapes)

salt and freshly ground black pepper

SAUCE

350g (12 oz) best butcher's very lean, high-meat content, pork sausages

a little olive oil

3 cloves garlic, crushed

1 small red chilli, seeded and finely chopped

2 × 400g (14 oz) tins of chopped tomatoes

1 good tablespoon sun-dried tomato paste

1 level teaspoon freeze-dried basil

1 teaspoon caster sugar

TO FINISH

50g (2 oz) Parmesan, coarsely grated

3 tablespoons chopped fresh parsley

1 Make long slits in each sausage and remove the skins. Measure a little oil into a non-stick frying pan, and fry the garlic and sausagemeat on the Boiling Plate. Mash down and brown well, then stir in the remaining sauce ingredients. Bring to the boil, cover and transfer to the Simmering Oven for 30–40 minutes. Check the seasoning.

2 Meanwhile, add the pasta to a large pan of boiling salted water. Bring to the boil on the Boiling Plate, then cover and cook on the Simmering Plate until al dente, about 12 minutes. Drain and set to one side.

3 Toss the sauce with the drained pasta, adding half the cheese. Scatter the parsley and remaining Parmesan over individual portions.

TO PREPARE AHEAD   Make the sauce ahead and chill for up to 3 days.

TO FREEZE   Freeze the sauce at the end of stage 1 for up to 1 month.

TO THAW   Thaw at room temperature for about 5 hours.

TO REHEAT   Reheat the sauce on the Simmering Plate whilst the pasta is cooking.

TO COOK IN A CONVENTIONAL OVEN   Cook on the hob in the usual way.

TAGLIATELLE CON POMODORI

A wonderfully healthy pasta dish, with no cream in sight! The anchovies do not overpower the sauce, but give the flavour depth.

Serves 6

2 × 50g (2 oz) tins of anchovy fillets in olive oil, snipped with scissors (keep the oil)

350g (12 oz) onions, chopped

1 head of fennel, finely chopped

3 large cloves garlic, crushed

1 small red chilli, seeded and finely chopped

2 × 400g (14 oz) tins of chopped tomatoes

½ teaspoon caster sugar

salt and freshly ground black pepper

350g (12 oz) dried tagliatelle

1 teaspoon balsamic vinegar

3 tablespoons roughly chopped fresh flat-leaf parsley

100g (4 oz) pine kernels, lightly toasted (see page 83)

grated Parmesan

1 Heat the anchovy oil kept from the tin in a large frying pan on the Boiling Plate, then add the onion, fennel, garlic and chilli. Fry gently for 5 minutes, stirring from time to time, then cover and transfer to the Simmering Oven for approximately 15 minutes until the onion is soft.

2 Return to the Boiling Plate, add the tomatoes, chopped anchovies, sugar, salt and pepper and bring back to the boil. Cover again and return to the Simmering Oven for a further 10 minutes.

3 Add the pasta to a large pan of boiling salted water. Bring to the boil on the Boiling Plate, then cover and cook on the Simmering Plate until al dente, about 12 minutes. Drain and mix in with the sauce. You may need to thin the sauce down a little with some boiling water. (This is a generous amount of sauce so you may like to chill some for another day.)

4 Add the balsamic vinegar, then sprinkle with parsley and warm pine kernels. Serve with freshly grated Parmesan.

TO PREPARE AHEAD   Chill the sauce for up to 3 days.

TO FREEZE   Freeze the sauce at the end of stage 2 for up to 1 month.

TO THAW   Thaw at room temperature for about 5 hours.

TO REHEAT   Reheat the sauce until boiling whilst the pasta is cooking.

TO COOK IN A CONVENTIONAL OVEN   Cook the sauce on the hob in the usual way for about 30 minutes.

PASTA AL FRESCO

This is wonderful to eat out of doors for a summer lunch. Go carefully with the salt as Parmesan and dry-cured ham may both be fairly salty already.

Serves 6

350g (12 oz) dried pasta of choice
salt and freshly ground black pepper
1 dessertspoon olive oil
175g (6 oz) Black Forest ham, cut very
  thin and snipped into pieces (or any
  cured or air-dried ham)

300ml (10 fl oz) double cream
100g (4 oz) Parmesan, coarsely grated or
  shaved
a handful of fresh parsley, chopped

1 Heat a large serving dish (a good idea especially if you want to serve the pasta out of doors).

2 Add the pasta to a large pan of boiling salted water. Bring to the boil on the Boiling Plate, then cover and cook on the Simmering Plate for about 12 minutes, until al dente.

3 While the pasta is cooking, measure the oil into a deep, non-stick frying pan and cook the ham quickly for 2–3 minutes on the Boiling Plate until just beginning to crisp. Lift out the crisp ham and keep warm.

4 When the pasta is cooked, drain well and put to one side. Bring the cream to the boil in the empty pan, season well, then return the pasta to the pan. Add the Parmesan, half the ham and most of the parsley. Check seasoning and toss thoroughly.

5 Turn into the hot serving dish, and scatter with the remaining parsley and reserved ham. Serve at once, with a green salad.

TO PREPARE AHEAD   This is such a quick dish to prepare that it is not really worth preparing ahead.

TO FREEZE   Not suitable.

TO COOK IN A CONVENTIONAL OVEN   Cook on the hob in the usual way.

SMOKED BACON AND MUSHROOM RISOTTO

This is a perfect supper dish, served perhaps with a good warm bread such as ciabatta or focaccia. It's essential to choose small courgettes because you then get the bright green colour which livens up the risotto.

Serves 4–6

2 tablespoons olive oil

1 large onion, coarsely chopped

2 cloves garlic, crushed

1 red pepper, seeded and finely chopped

175g (6 oz) button mushrooms, sliced

250g (9 oz) arborio or other risotto rice

900ml (30 fl oz) chicken stock, home-made if possible, hot

salt and freshly ground black pepper

225g (8 oz) smoked streaky bacon, cut into strips

275g (10 oz) small courgettes, diced

25g (1 oz) butter

50g (2 oz) Parmesan, grated, and a few shaved slices

chopped fresh parsley

1 Heat the oil in a large non-stick frying pan on the Boiling Plate, add the onion, garlic and red pepper, and sauté for a few minutes. Toss in the mushrooms and cook for a further minute.

2 Add the rice and stir for 2 minutes. Pour in 750ml (25 fl oz) of boiling stock and season.

3 Cover with the lid and transfer to the Simmering Oven for 25 minutes. Check and stir once during this time, bringing back to the boil on the Boiling Plate, and adding more stock if necessary.

4 Fry and brown the bacon on the Boiling Plate in a large non-stick frying pan. Remove and put on to a plate. Add the courgettes to the fat in the pan and fry until just tender. Put to one side with the bacon.

5 Test the rice: it should be soft on the outside but still have a little bite in the centre. Return to the Boiling Plate to reduce if there is excess liquid. Add the butter, grated Parmesan, the bacon and courgettes. Check the seasoning and serve sprinkled with chopped parsley and shavings of fresh Parmesan if liked.

TO PREPARE AHEAD   Complete to the end of stage 4 about 8 hours ahead, and chill.

TO FREEZE   Not suitable.

TO REHEAT   Reheat the rice, etc., on the Boiling Plate then add the butter, Parmesan, cooked bacon and courgettes. Add the parsley and Parmesan shavings.

TO COOK IN A CONVENTIONAL OVEN   Cook on the hob in the usual way.

VEGETABLES

Vegetables are very versatile, capable of being served as first course, main course or hot to serve with fish or meat. The Aga is just as versatile in the way in which it can be used to *cook* those same vegetables, whether on the hotplates, or in the ovens. They can be steamed, poached, boiled or fried, stir-fried or grilled, baked or roasted.

There are several recipes here which, to me, demonstrate the ability of the Aga to produce magnificent results. My Aga way of cooking vegetables in advance is to blanch them, blasting them with heat in the Roasting Oven at the last minute so that they are cooked to perfection. Another couple of recipes tell you how to roast vegetables, a delicious modern idea, using our very British roots as well as a selection of Mediterranean vegetables (but you can actually use any vegetable you like). I've described too how to dry tomatoes and mushrooms, two 'new' and exciting ingredients of current cooking which I now find invaluable. The gentle heat of the Aga is ideal for this.

I've also written quite a few recipes using potatoes, simply because people like them, and still want them as an accompaniment for the main course. I hope you'll like the choice here.

SHIITAKE MUSHROOM STIR-FRY V

All the ingredients can be prepared ahead in the morning, then stir-fried when everyone is ready.

Serves 4–6

2 generous tablespoons vegetable oil

1 × 2.5cm (1 in) piece of fresh root ginger, cut into fine julienne strips

2 cloves garlic, crushed

4 spring onions, cut diagonally into thin slices

6 sticks celery, cut diagonally into slices

100g (4 oz) mangetout, trimmed and cut diagonally into short diamonds

½ red pepper, seeded and cut into strips lengthways

150g (5 oz) fresh beansprouts

150g (5 oz) shiitake (or oyster) mushrooms, thinly sliced

1 tablespoon soy sauce

1 tablespoon oyster sauce (if available)

1 Heat the oil in a large non-stick deep frying pan on the Boiling Plate. When this oil is really hot, put in the ginger and garlic, stir well and add the spring onions, celery, mangetout and red pepper. Continue stirring for 2–3 minutes. I use two wooden spatulas.

2 Add the beansprouts and mushrooms, the soy sauce and lastly, if available, the oyster sauce. Season well. Serve immediately.

TO PREPARE AHEAD Prepare the ingredients ahead of time, in the morning, say. Keep, covered, in a cool place until ready to stir-fry.

TO FREEZE Not suitable.

TO COOK IN A CONVENTIONAL OVEN Cook on the hob in the usual way.

PROTECTING FROM SPLATTERS

When stir-frying or grilling something on the Boiling Plate, cover the opened lid with a tea-towel to protect it from splatters. Then remove as it would scorch when you put the lid down.

DAUPHINOISE POTATO CAKES

A wonderful way to serve up potatoes that can be prepared ahead and reheated to serve. Traditionally dauphinoise potatoes are made with cream which is delicious but rather rich. If this is how you like them, add 450ml (15 fl oz) double cream instead of the stock. It is much easier to cut through the potato with the cutter when completely cold, i.e. straight from the fridge.

Makes 12 cakes, to serve about 8

a little melted butter

1.4kg (3 lb) old potatoes, washed

salt and freshly ground black pepper

1 clove garlic, crushed

450ml (15 fl oz) chicken stock, or water
and 2 chicken stock cubes

a little chopped fresh parsley

1 Line the base and sides of a small roasting tin with greaseproof or non-stick baking paper, and brush generously with melted butter.

2 Peel and thinly slice the potatoes. Arrange the slices in the roasting tin, seasoning between the layers. Blend the crushed garlic with the stock and pour some in between the layers and some over the top.

3 Bake on the lowest set of runners in the Roasting Oven, covered with buttered paper, for about 45 minutes. Turn around half way through the cooking time. When the potatoes are tender, remove from the oven and leave to become completely cold.

4 Using a 6.5cm (2½ in) diameter scone cutter, stamp out twelve round potato cakes. If the scone cutter is warm, it will slice through the potatoes more easily. (All the rather tatty-looking odd pieces of potato left over can be put in a shallow buttered dish, levelled and dotted with butter, then browned in the Roasting Oven for about 15 minutes and served for supper.)

5 Arrange the round cakes on well-buttered Lift-Off paper on a baking sheet, brush each with butter and reheat for 12 minutes in the top of the Roasting Oven until hot and brown. Scatter with chopped parsley.

TO PREPARE AHEAD Cut the potatoes out as in stage 4, put on well-buttered Lift-Off paper on a baking sheet, cover with clingfilm and keep in the fridge for up to 24 hours.

TO FREEZE These potato cakes do not freeze successfully.

TO REHEAT As above at stage 5.

TO COOK IN A CONVENTIONAL OVEN Cook the potatoes in the roasting tin in the oven, preheated to 200°C/400°F/Gas mark 6, for about 1 hour. Allow to cool, cut into rounds, brush with butter and reheat at 220°C/425°F/Gas mark 7 for about 15 minutes until hot and golden brown on top.

SWISS POTATOES V

This recipe can be cooked in one large dish for family occasions, when the cooking time will of course be longer, about 25 minutes. For a dinner party, make either one-portion-sized mounds or smaller ones if liked. Cook ahead then reheat for 5 minutes in the Roasting Oven.

Serves 6–8

4 medium potatoes, Desirée or King Edwards	1 large onion, roughly chopped
salt and freshly ground black pepper	40g (1½ oz) butter
	vegetable oil

1 Boil the potatoes whole in their skins in salted water on the Boiling Plate until only just done. Drain and leave to cool.

2 Bring the chopped onion to the boil in salted water on the Boiling Plate, cover and transfer to the floor of the Simmering Oven for 10 minutes. Drain really well, then return to the saucepan and add the butter.

3 Peel and coarsely grate the cold potatoes, then combine with the onion and butter. Season well. Divide into about twelve one-portion-sized mounds, and place either on Lift-Off paper or on a greased baking sheet. Bake on the floor of the Roasting Oven until pale golden brown, about 20 minutes.

TO PREPARE AHEAD Cook ahead to the end of stage 4. Cool and store in the fridge for no longer than a day.

TO FREEZE Freeze at the end of stage 3, for up to 6 weeks.

TO THAW Not necessary. Cook from frozen for about 10–15 minutes. You may need to cover them with foil if getting too brown.

TO REHEAT Reheat for about 5 minutes in the Roasting Oven, on the second set of runners.

TO COOK IN A CONVENTIONAL OVEN Cook in the oven preheated to 200°C/400°F/Gas mark 6, for about 40 minutes or until crisp and golden.

THE VERY BEST MASHED POTATO ^V

Everyone loves a good mash, and this really is good. If there is any left, just spread it in a shallow ovenproof dish, dot with butter and reheat in the Roasting Oven for about 25 minutes until piping hot and brown.

Serves 6

900g (2 lb) old potatoes	about 8 tablespoons hot milk
salt and freshly ground black pepper	50–75g (2–3 oz) butter

1 Peel the potatoes, cut into even sizes, cover with cold salted water and a lid and bring to the boil on the Boiling Plate. Boil for 5 minutes, drain thoroughly, cover again and place in the Simmering Oven until tender – about 40 minutes, longer if the pieces are large.

2 Draw the potatoes to one side of the pan, add the milk and butter, allow to almost boil on the Simmering Plate, and add seasoning. Mash the potatoes well, heat for a few moments and spoon into a serving dish.

3 Cover with clingfilm and keep warm for up to 30 minutes if necessary.

HERB MASH Add 3 tablespoons coarsely chopped fresh parsley and chives to the mashed potato. (The flavour of the herbs develops if the potatoes are kept warm for up to 30 minutes.) Add good olive oil instead of butter for a Mediterranean flavour.

MUSTARD MASH Add 4 tablespoons grain mustard to the mashed potato.

MANGO AND SPRING ONION MASH Add about 4 tablespoons of a mixture of mango chutney (chopping up the big bits first) and chopped spring onion to the mashed potato.

TO PREPARE AHEAD Complete stage 2. Spread in a shallow ovenproof dish, dot with butter, cool and chill for up to 6 hours.

TO FREEZE Not suitable.

TO REHEAT Reheat on the grid shelf near to the top of the Roasting Oven for about 25 minutes to brown.

TO COOK IN A CONVENTIONAL OVEN Use the hob in the usual way.

BAKED FENNEL WITH RED PEPPERS AND PARMESAN V

This combination of Mediterranean vegetables goes well with steaks and lamb.

Serves 6

3 heads of fennel

salt and freshly ground black pepper

½ red pepper, seeded and cut into
    pencil-thin strips

1–2 tablespoons olive oil

50–75g (2–3 oz) Parmesan, grated

a little paprika

1 Remove the tops of the fennel and cut each bulb into four wedges. Cook in boiling salted water on the Boiling Plate for about 10 minutes, then drain and refresh in cold water.

2 Toss the fennel and strips of pepper in olive oil until all are coated well.

3 Arrange the fennel quarters in an ovenproof dish, placing strips of pepper in between. Season with salt and pepper, sprinkle with grated Parmesan, and dust with paprika.

4 Bake on the floor of the Roasting Oven for 15–20 minutes until the fennel is tender.

TO PREPARE AHEAD Prepare up to the end of stage 3. Cover and keep in the fridge for up to 12 hours before baking.

TO FREEZE Not suitable.

TO COOK IN A CONVENTIONAL OVEN Cook in the oven preheated to 200°C/400°F/ Gas mark 6 for 15–20 minutes until the fennel is tender.

BROWNING

If you need something to brown quickly – toasted savouries to have with drinks, or vegetables – sprinkle a little paprika on top before you pop into the top of the Roasting Oven. It adds to the taste too!

A COLLECTION OF CHEF'S VEGETABLES V

All the vegetables are cooked to perfection ahead, even the day before if it suits you! This means that you can wash up all the pans ahead and there is no last-minute panic. Keep the vegetables covered in the cool until they are needed, then blast with heat in the Roasting Oven until piping hot, but not re-cooked. Vary the vegetables as you wish. Do potato mash instead of new if you like. Puréed vegetables – e.g. celeriac, carrot and swede – do well, and red cabbage is delicious too.

To save having too many pans of boiling water, I remove the vegetables with a slotted spoon and re-use the same boiling water.

Serves 6–8

about 900g (2 lb) baby new potatoes, washed (scraped if you like)	about 225g (8 oz) young green beans, trimmed
salt and freshly ground black pepper	about 225g (8 oz) new whole baby carrots, trimmed
about 225g (8 oz) prepared leeks, washed and thinly sliced	about 225g (8 oz) broccoli sprigs
	about 25g (1 oz) butter, melted

1 Bring the potatoes to the boil in salted water on the Boiling Plate, cover and simmer for 2 minutes. Drain off the water, cover with a lid and transfer to the floor of the Simmering Oven for about 30 minutes or until just tender. Refresh in cold water, drain well.

2 Add the leeks to fresh boiling salted water as above and cook for about 2 minutes, then remove from the water with a slotted spoon. Refresh in cold water, then drain well on kitchen paper.

3 Add the beans to the same boiling salted water and cook as above for about 4–5 minutes until al dente. Drain from the water, refresh with cold water, then drain well on kitchen paper.

4 Add the carrots to the same boiling salted water and cook as above for about 5 minutes depending on size, until just tender. Drain from the water, refresh in cold water, then drain well on kitchen paper.

5 Add the broccoli sprigs to the same boiling salted water and cook as above for about 2–3 minutes, until just tender. Drain from the water, refresh in cold water, then drain well on kitchen paper.

6 Toss each batch of vegetables, individually, in a little melted butter and season well. Arrange in a large flat ovenproof dish, and cover tightly with buttered foil.

7 Place the dish on the floor of the Roasting Oven for about 20 minutes until the vegetables are steaming and you can hear the butter sizzle. Serve at once. Don't attempt to keep them hot: they will lose their perfect colour and crispness.

TO PREPARE AHEAD   Prepare up to a day ahead to the end of stage 6.

TO FREEZE   Not suitable.

TO COOK IN A CONVENTIONAL OVEN   Cook the vegetables on the hob in the normal way, as indicated to the end of stage 6. Then cook in the oven, preheated to 220°C/425°F/Gas mark 7, for about 25–30 minutes until the vegetables are piping hot.

ENGLISH ROAST VEGETABLES V

Sweet potatoes are a welcome addition to our usual choice of root vegetables, as are the squashes. They are very apt to stick to the tin, so beware. Cut them into larger pieces than the other vegetables as they take less time to cook.

Serves 6

3 large onions
6 medium potatoes
3 large carrots
3 large parsnips
about 550g (1¼ lb) squash, such as
   butternut, or sweet potatoes
   (unpeeled weight)

2 fat cloves garlic, crushed (optional)
about 3 tablespoons goose fat, duck fat
  or oil
salt and freshly ground black pepper

1 Peel the onions, leaving the root end intact so the onion holds together. Cut the onions into quarters.

2 Peel the potatoes, carrots, parsnips and squash or sweet potato and cut the potatoes and carrots into small chunks, the other vegetables into large chunks. Toss together with the garlic (if using) and fat in a bowl, then season well. Turn into the large roasting tin.

3 Cook in the Roasting Oven on the floor, turning after a few minutes to prevent them sticking to the tin. Turn as each side browns and cook until all the vegetables are tender and tinged with brown, about 45 minutes, depending on the size and thickness of the vegetables.

TO PREPARE AHEAD   A day ahead, complete to the end of stage 3, but under-cook the vegetables by about 20 minutes.

TO FREEZE   Not suitable.

TO REHEAT   Slide the roasting tin on to the floor of the Roasting Oven and reheat for about 15 minutes until the vegetables are tender, golden and piping hot.

TO COOK IN A CONVENTIONAL OVEN   Cook in the oven preheated to 230°C/450°F/ Gas mark 8 for about 1 hour until the vegetables are tender and brown.

ROASTED MEDITERRANEAN VEGETABLES V

Alter the vegetables as you like – fennel and red onions work well too. The dish is very good with lamb. If you want to serve the vegetables cold in summer with salad, add a little balsamic vinegar.

Serves 6

2 large onions	I large aubergine
2 yellow peppers, seeded	2 fat cloves garlic
2 red peppers, seeded	3 tablespoons olive oil
4 medium courgettes	salt and freshly ground black pepper

1 First prepare the vegetables. Quarter the onions, cut the peppers into large pieces, thickly slice the courgettes and cut the aubergine into 2.5cm (1 in) chunks. Crush the garlic.

2 Toss the onion in 1 tablespoon of the olive oil, sprinkle with salt and pepper and turn into the large roasting tin. Put on the floor of the Roasting Oven for about 20 minutes until beginning to soften and brown.

3 Add the rest of the prepared vegetables and the garlic to the tin with the remaining oil, stir to coat the vegetables in the oil and return the tin to the floor of the Roasting Oven for about 20–30 minutes until the vegetables are tender and well browned. Turn the vegetables over occasionally with a wooden spatula to ensure that they brown evenly.

TO PREPARE AHEAD   Complete to the end of stage 3, but under-cook the vegetables slightly. Cool, cover and keep in the fridge for up to a day ahead.

TO FREEZE   Not suitable.

TO REHEAT   Reheat on the floor of the Roasting Oven for 10–15 minutes.

TO COOK IN A CONVENTIONAL OVEN   Cook in the oven, preheated to 230°C/450°F/ Gas mark 8 for about 30–40 minutes, cooking the onion first for about 10 minutes, until all the vegetables are well browned and tender.

CUCUMBER AND MINTED PEAS V

A very summery accompaniment, good with fish, this is a quick alternative to ordinary petits pois. Do not over-cook the cucumber, or it will become watery and tasteless.

Serves 4

1 cucumber	25g (1 oz) butter
salt and freshly ground black pepper	2 teaspoons finely chopped fresh mint
300g (11 oz) frozen peas or fresh	
garden peas	

1 Peel the cucumber using a potato peeler, cut in half lengthways, scoop out the seeds using a small teaspoon, and cut into thick batons (half-moon shapes).

2 Bring a smallish saucepan of salted water to the boil on the Boiling Plate and blanch the cucumber for 1 minute. Scoop out the cucumber using a draining spoon. This water can now be used to cook the peas according to the directions on the packet.

3 Whilst the peas are boiling, melt the butter in a frying pan on the Boiling Plate and sauté the blanched and drained cucumber for 2–3 minutes. Add the drained peas, chopped mint and black pepper. Transfer to a serving dish.

TO PREPARE AHEAD Blanch the cucumber ahead of time, in the morning, say. Drain and refresh in cold water.

TO FREEZE Not suitable.

TO COOK IN A CONVENTIONAL OVEN Cook on the hob in the normal way.

FRAGRANT RICE ᵛ

This spicy rice mixture goes well with chicken and pork sausages, or it can be served on its own or as part of a vegetarian meal.

Serves 6

350g (12 oz) easy-cook or par-boiled
   rice (e.g. Uncle Ben's)
500ml (18 fl oz) cold water
salt and freshly ground black pepper
4 tablespoons good olive oil
2 teaspoons medium curry powder

about 4 sweet red onions (225g/8 oz),
   thinly sliced
2 cloves garlic, crushed
2 aubergines, cut into cubes
2 red peppers, seeded and sliced
2 tablespoons soy sauce
2 tablespoons chopped fresh parsley

1 Measure the rice, water and 1 teaspoon salt into a pan, bring to the boil on the Boiling Plate, cover, then transfer to the floor of the Simmering Oven for about 15 minutes until tender and all the liquid is absorbed.

2 Heat the oil in a generous-sized pan, add the curry powder, onion and garlic and cook on the Boiling Plate for 2–3 minutes. Add the aubergine and red pepper to the pan. Cook for a further 3 minutes, then cover and transfer to the floor of the Simmering Oven for 10 minutes until tender.

3 Return the pan to the Boiling Plate, and boil off any excess juices. Stir in the cooked rice and soy sauce and season well. Scatter with parsley before serving.

TO PREPARE AHEAD Cook and turn into a buttered shallow dish. Cool and cover loosely with foil, and keep in the fridge for up to 24 hours.

TO FREEZE Not suitable.

TO REHEAT Cook on the grid shelf towards the top of the Roasting Oven for about 15 minutes still covered with foil, until piping hot. Scatter with parsley to serve.

TO COOK IN A CONVENTIONAL OVEN Cook on the hob in the usual way.

APRICOT COUSCOUS TIMBALES V

If it frightens you to prepare timbale moulds you can very easily serve this dish as a salad, with some salad dressing. The clingfilm lining the moulds makes them easier to turn out, when cold, but if you want to serve the timbales hot, simply grease the moulds. You can use ramekins or tea cups to save you buying new moulds.

Serves 6

olive oil

300ml (10 fl oz) vegetable stock

100g (4 oz) fine asparagus tips, halved

175g (6 oz) couscous

100g (4 oz) dried ready-soaked apricots, finely chopped

2 tablespoons chopped fresh mint

2 tablespoons chopped fresh parsley

75g (3 oz) salted cashew nuts

salt and freshly ground black pepper

1 Line six timbale moulds with clingfilm if serving cold, or oil the moulds if serving hot.

2 Bring the stock to the boil on the Boiling Plate, then add the asparagus tips to cook for about 3 minutes until al dente.

3 Put the couscous into a large heatproof bowl with the apricots and stand a colander over the top. Drain the stock and asparagus over the colander so the stock covers the couscous. Cover with a tea-towel for about 5 minutes until all the liquid is absorbed. Immediately refresh the asparagus in cold water and leave to drain.

4 Mix the mint and parsley with 3 tablespoons of the oil.

5 Once the stock is all absorbed into the couscous, fluff up with a fork and stir in the cashew nuts, mint, parsley, oil, salt and pepper and finally the asparagus. Stir so that all the ingredients are evenly distributed.

6 Press the couscous mixture firmly into the timbale moulds. If time allows, leave them covered in clingfilm in the fridge. Carefully turn out and remove the clingfilm top and mould lining. Serve immediately.

7 To serve hot, reheat in the timbale moulds covered in foil on the second set of runners in the Roasting Oven for about 6 minutes. Alternatively, reheat in the Simmering Oven for about 15 minutes. (Those in the Simmering Oven can be lined with clingfilm.)

TO PREPARE AHEAD Make up to 12 hours ahead, when they are even nicer, as the herb flavours infuse into the couscous.

TO FREEZE Not suitable.

TO REHEAT   As above in stage 7.

TO COOK IN A CONVENTIONAL OVEN   Heat in the timbale moulds in boiling water in a frying pan for about 10 minutes. The water should come half way up the tins.

AGA-DRIED FIELD MUSHROOMS V

Choose smallish, dry, perfect mushrooms. Do not use aged mushrooms with holes in them.

1 Remove and discard stalks, then slice the mushrooms with a sharp knife into thin slices. Very small mushrooms can be just cut in half.

2 Arrange the slices on Lift-Off paper or non-stick baking parchment on a baking sheet. (Putting a lining on the baking sheet is not essential, it just saves on the washing up!)

3 ▮ Put a dish cloth on top of the lid of the Simmering Plate and stand the baking sheet on top. Leave for about 48 hours until the mushrooms are brittle and dry. This may be inconvenient during the day. If so, put them to one side and just dry them at night. Obviously this will take longer.

▮▮ Stand the baking sheet on the Warming Plate to the left of the Boiling Plate and leave for about 48 hours until the mushrooms are brittle and dry.

4 Store in clean lidded glass jars and use before the season comes round again.

AGA-DRIED TOMATOES V

In Italy they usually sun-dry plum tomatoes. I suggest you dry whatever variety you grow that are not needed for salads or cooking. I add a little sugar to counteract the lack of taste of Italian sunshine!

Makes about 450g (1 lb)

12 ripe, firm tomatoes	olive oil
sea salt and freshly ground black pepper	garlic, thyme and basil (optional flavourings)
a dash of caster sugar	

1 Remove the stalks then cut the tomatoes in half, and remove the seeds with a teaspoon. Lay the tomatoes cut side up on Lift-Off paper on a baking sheet, and sprinkle with salt and pepper and a dash of sugar. Drizzle a little olive oil over them.

2 Place in the Simmering Oven for approximately 6 hours. The tomatoes should reduce to half their original size but not turn brown. Turn them over for the last hour. The finished tomatoes should be firm. Keep an eye on them.

3 When the tomatoes are cool, place in a jar with the flavourings (if using) and cover with olive oil. This can be stored in the fridge for 3 months if well sealed. Expect the oil to become cloudy.

GLASSES

Put glasses or a decanter upside down on a cloth at the back of the Aga, and they will dry off beautifully, with no smears.

PUDDINGS

Most of those who come to my Aga workshops are very interested in cooking puddings, whether hot or cold. The Aga somehow invites you to use its constant heat to poach some fruits, bake a cheesecake, tart or pie, or a delicate meringue.

Pastry puddings, particularly tarts, are perfectly designed for the Aga. By putting the porcelain flan dish or tart tin on the floor of the Roasting Oven, the direct heat from below will crisp and brown the bottom pastry, while the radiant heat in the oven will cook and brown the remaining pastry and set the filling. It's such a relief after so many years of baking pastry blind, which is time-consuming and can be troublesome.

Other recipes may be familiar, but have been adapted for the Aga. For instance Îles Flottantes (see opposite) – 'floating islands' of glossy meringue – are usually poached in milk and then arranged on top of a separately cooked sea of custard. Here both are baked together in the warmth of the Simmering Oven, and they taste wonderful!

Many of these puddings can be prepared and cooked ahead of time, which is always useful when you are organising a lunch or dinner party. If you know one of the courses is ready, needing no more than a few minutes' reheating in the oven, you can relax a bit more and happily concentrate on everything else.

ÎLES FLOTTANTES V

Such an ideal recipe for the Aga as the meringues are poached in the Simmering Oven. Serve this with a red fruit salad – the colours look magnificent – or simply on its own.

Serves 8

butter	600ml (20 fl oz) milk
3 eggs, separated	½ teaspoon vanilla extract
200g (7 oz) caster sugar	I heaped teaspoon cornflour

1 Grease a shallow 23–25cm (9–10 in) shallow ovenproof dish with butter. The dish must have a large top surface to accommodate the meringues.

2 Whisk the egg whites at full speed in an electric mixer for 1 minute, then add 175g (6 oz) of the sugar gradually over several minutes, keeping the whisk at full speed, until the meringue is stiff and glossy.

3 Bring the milk to the boil.

4 In a separate bowl mix the egg yolks, the remaining caster sugar, the vanilla and cornflour. Using a balloon whisk, pour on the boiling milk very slowly and whisk all the time. Return the custard to the heat and cook gently until the froth disappears and the custard is lightly thickened. Pour the custard into the prepared dish.

5 Using 2 tablespoons, make oval shapes from the meringue and arrange these on top of the custard. The mixture should make about ten meringues.

6 Transfer the meringues and custard to the Simmering Oven and bake for 15–20 minutes, or until the meringues are set and no longer sticky when lightly pressed with the finger. Serve warm, perhaps with a red fruit salad.

TO PREPARE AHEAD Can be cooked, cooled, covered and kept in the fridge for up to 2 days. The meringues will shrink slightly during this time.

TO FREEZE Not suitable.

TO COOK IN A CONVENTIONAL OVEN Bake the custard and meringues in the oven preheated to 160°C/325°F/Gas mark 3 for about 20 minutes, until the meringues are set and no longer sticky.

LIME MERINGUE ROULADE V

A meringue roulade is quicker and easier to make than a lemon meringue pie, and is just as popular. It freezes extremely well.

Makes 8–10 slices

5 egg whites	FILLING
275g (10 oz) caster sugar	300ml (10 fl oz) double cream
50g (2 oz) flaked almonds	grated rind and juice of 1 small lime
	2 generous tablespoons lime or
	lemon curd

1 Line a 33 × 23cm (13 × 9 in) Swiss roll tin with greased non-stick baking paper. Secure the corners with four paper clips, or staple each corner.

2 First make the meringue. Whisk the egg whites in an electric mixer on full speed until very stiff. Gradually add the sugar, a teaspoon at a time, still on high speed, whisking well between each addition. Whisk until very, very stiff and shiny, and all the sugar has been added.

3 Spread the meringue mixture into the prepared tin and sprinkle with the almonds.

4 ⦂ Put the tin on the grid shelf on the floor of the Roasting Oven with the cold plain shelf on the second set of runners and bake for about 8 minutes until pale golden. Then transfer to the Simmering Oven, and bake the roulade for a further 15 minutes until slightly crisp and firm to the touch. The roulade does expand, so take care of the edges when transferring.

⦂⦂ Put the tin on the grid shelf on the floor of the Baking Oven and bake for about 8 minutes until pale golden. Then transfer to the Simmering Oven, and bake the roulade for a further 15 minutes until slightly crisp and firm to the touch.

5 Remove the meringue from the oven and turn almond side down on to a sheet of non-stick baking paper. Remove the paper from the base of the cooked meringue and allow to cool for about 10 minutes.

6 Lightly whip the cream, add the lime rind and juice, and fold in the lime or lemon curd. Spread evenly over the meringue. Make an indentation 1cm ($\frac{1}{2}$ in) in on the long side with a knife, then roll up the meringue fairly tightly from the long end to form a roulade, allowing the paper to help you roll. It is essential to roll tightly and firmly at the beginning. Expect the roulade to crack, it is part of its charm.

7 Wrap in non-stick baking paper and chill well before serving – with raspberries if liked.

TO PREPARE AHEAD   The roulade can be made the day before it is needed. Complete to the end of stage 6, wrap and keep in the fridge.

TO FREEZE   This roulade freezes well, stuffed and rolled, and so is perfect for entertaining. Wrap in foil and freeze for up to 2 months.

TO THAW   Thaw the roulade for about 8 hours in the fridge.

TO COOK IN A CONVENTIONAL OVEN   Cook the meringue in the oven preheated to 220°C/425°F/Gas mark 7 for about 12 minutes until golden. Then lower the oven temperature to 160°C/325°F/Gas mark 3 and bake for about a further 15 minutes until firm to the touch.

OPENING JARS

If you have a stubborn metal lid that won't come off a jar of pickle or jelly, open the Simmering Plate lid, and invert the jar directly on to the plate for a few moments. The metal will expand and the lid can be opened.

AUSTRIAN APRICOT AND ALMOND TART V

This tart looks wonderful when it is cooked as the pastry cover moulds itself to the shape of the apricots. If you're short of time, use a 500g (18 oz) packet of bought shortcrust pastry. Make with fresh apricots when in season and add sugar to taste. (A variation is to use fresh, stoned plums.) If you choose to use an ovenproof 25cm (10 in) fluted flan dish (rather than tin), the tart will take longer to cook.

Serves 8

PASTRY
275g (10 oz) plain flour
150g (5 oz) icing sugar
150g (5 oz) butter, cubed
1 egg

FILLING
175g (6 oz) almond paste or marzipan,
   coarsely grated
2 × 400g (14 oz) tins of halved apricots
   in natural juice

TO SERVE
icing sugar
cream or crème fraîche

1 Measure the flour, icing sugar and butter into a processor. Process until it resembles a crumble. Add the egg and process until the mixture holds together. Gather together on a floured table. Wrap in clingfilm and leave in the fridge for about 15 minutes.

2 Take off a little less than half the chilled pastry for the top and return to the fridge. Roll out the rest of the pastry to make a circle large enough to line a 25cm (10 in) fluted flan tin. The pastry is a bit on the soft side but patches up easily! Spread the grated almond paste over the base of the flan. Drain the apricots thoroughly and arrange on the base of the flan tin, cut side down. Roll out any trimmings with the remaining pastry for the lid. Damp the edge of the rim of the pastry in the flan tin. Lift the pastry over the top of the fruit, and press the two layers of pastry together, patching the edges if necessary. Stand on a metal baking sheet.

3 ● Bake on the floor of the Roasting Oven with the cold plain shelf on the second set of runners for about 20 minutes. Watch carefully. As the pastry is a sweet one, the edges will brown first, so cover with a piece of foil with a 20cm (8 in) circle taken out of the centre to make a ring just to cover the edges.
   ●● Bake on the floor of the Roasting Oven for 15 minutes. When the pastry is pale golden, transfer to the Baking Oven on the grid shelf on the floor, until a good golden colour, another 15 minutes. If the edges are becoming too brown, slip in the cold plain shelf above.

4 Sieve some icing sugar over before serving. Serve with cream or crème fraîche.

TO PREPARE AHEAD   The tart can be made, covered in clingfilm and kept in the fridge for up to 24 hours before baking. Allow the tart to stand at room temperature for about 20 minutes before baking.

TO FREEZE   Not suitable.

TO COOK IN A CONVENTIONAL OVEN   Place a flat heavy baking tray in the oven to preheat. Bake the tart in the oven, preheated to 180°C/350°F/Gas mark 4, for about 30–35 minutes or until pale golden.

APPLE AND ALMOND JALOUSIE V

Apples and almonds go well together, and the slit pastry topping looks good. It's quick and easy, and a proper pudding!

Serves 6–8

450g (1 lb) frozen puff pastry, defrosted
900g (2 lb) dessert apples
1 heaped tablespoon cornflour
2 tablespoons apricot jam
100g (4 oz) marzipan or almond paste, grated
plain flour

TOPPING
1 egg, beaten
25g (1 oz) flaked almonds
extra apricot jam, heated, to glaze

1 Cut the pastry in half. Roll one piece to a 28–30cm (11–12 in) circle and place on a baking sheet.

2 Peel, core and thinly slice the apples into a bowl, add the cornflour, apricot jam and grated marzipan, and mix well. Spoon this mixture on to the pastry circle, spreading to 1cm ($\frac{1}{2}$ in) from the edge.

3 Roll the second piece of pastry slightly larger than the first, cutting a circle of about 33–35cm (13–14 in). Lightly dust with flour, fold in half and, with a sharp knife, cut across the fold at 5mm ($\frac{1}{4}$ in) intervals, but not right to the outer edges, leaving a border of about 2.5–4cm (1–1$\frac{1}{2}$ in).

4 Brush the outer edge of the first circle with beaten egg. Open out the folded pastry and press down on the egg, then seal the edges together. Glaze the jalousie with the remaining beaten egg, and sprinkle with the flaked almonds.

5 ⁚ Bake on the floor of the Roasting Oven for about 15 minutes, until pale golden brown. Slide the cold plain shelf on to the second set of runners and continue to bake for a further 10 minutes or until the apple is tender.

⁚⁚ Bake on the floor of the Roasting Oven for about 15 minutes or until pale golden brown, then transfer to the grid shelf on the floor of the Baking Oven for 15 minutes until the apple is tender.

6 Brush with melted apricot jam as a glaze. Serve hot with cream or crème fraîche.

TO PREPARE AHEAD Complete stage 5 and glaze, cool and put in the fridge for up to 24 hours.

TO FREEZE Cool, wrap and freeze for up to 1 month.

TO THAW Thaw at room temperature for about 12 hours.

TO REHEAT Place on the grid shelf on the floor of the Roasting Oven for about 10 minutes until piping hot. If getting too brown, slide the cold plain shelf on to the second set of runners.

TO COOK IN A CONVENTIONAL OVEN Bake at 220°C/425°F/Gas mark 7 for about 30 minutes, covering with foil if it is getting too brown.

ICE-CREAM PLUM PUDDING V

Not exactly an Aga recipe, but it cannot be left out of the book! If you can see flecks of butter or fat in the mincemeat, heat until the fat has melted, then cool before adding to the cream.

Serves 8–10

1 × 450g (1 lb) jar of vegetarian suet-free mincemeat	4 eggs
	300ml (10 fl oz) double cream
3 tablespoons brandy	100g (4 oz) caster sugar

1 Mix the mincemeat and brandy together.

2 Separate the eggs. Place the yolks in a small bowl and mix until well blended. Whisk the cream until it forms soft peaks. Using an electric mixer, whisk the egg whites on fast speed until stiff, then gradually add the sugar a teaspoonful at a time. You may need to scrape down the sides of the bowl from time to time.

3 Fold the egg yolks and cream into the meringue, followed by the brandy and mincemeat.

4 Turn the ice-cream mixture into a 2 litre (70 fl oz) pudding basin, cover and freeze overnight. Delicious served with a warm Toffee Sauce or a Brandy and Raisin Sauce (see overleaf).

TO PREPARE AHEAD The ice-cream can be frozen for up to 1 month.

TOFFEE SAUCE V

The children especially enjoy this sauce, and it disappears from the jar so quickly that I keep it in the fridge!

Makes about 450g (1 lb)

50g (2 oz) butter
75g (3 oz) caster sugar
50g (2 oz) light muscovado sugar

150g (5 oz) golden syrup
1 × 170g (6 oz) tin of evaporated milk

1 Put the butter, sugars and syrup in a pan and heat gently on the Simmering Plate until melted and liquid. Transfer to the Boiling Plate so the mixture boils gently for 5 minutes.

2 Remove the pan from the heat and gradually stir in the evaporated milk. The sauce is now ready and can be served hot or warm, or dolloped on cold.

TO PREPARE AHEAD Keeps in the fridge for 1 month.

BRANDY AND RAISIN SAUCE V

This is divine on any good vanilla or coffee ice-cream.

Makes about 450g (1 lb)

225g (8 oz) granulated sugar
6 tablespoons water

225g (8 oz) raisins
75ml (2½ fl oz) brandy

1 Combine the sugar and water in a medium-sized pan on the Simmering Plate, and leave over a low heat until the sugar is completely dissolved, stirring.

2 When the syrup is completely clear, stir in the raisins and continue to heat until they are hot. Remove the pan from the heat and add the brandy.

3 Cool and pour into two clean screw-top jars. Leave to plump up the raisins for at least 24 hours.

TO PREPARE AHEAD This sauce will keep indefinitely. If it crystallises in the jar just reheat it in a pan until the crystals are dissolved.

MANGO DELICE V

This is a very quick light dessert which can be made ahead of time, or frozen. If you do not want to make individual ramekins, use this recipe to fill an 18cm (7 in) china dish. Serve straight from the fridge so it is firm, garnished perhaps with lemon balm or mint leaves.

Serves 8

BISCUIT BASE
10 Hobnob biscuits, crushed
50g (2 oz) butter, melted

MANGO SAUCE
1 ripe mango, skinned and stoned
2 tablespoons icing sugar to taste

DELICE
1 small mango, skinned and stoned
300ml (10 fl oz) pouring double cream
1 × 400g (14 oz) tin of condensed milk
juice of 4 lemons

1 Grease and line eight small ramekins with clingfilm.

2 Mix together the crushed biscuits with the melted butter until well blended, and set aside.

3 For the delice filling, put the mango in a processor and whizz until smooth. Pour in the cream and condensed milk. Still whizzing, gradually pour in the lemon juice until the mixture thickens. Remove the blade and spoon into the ramekins.

4 Top each ramekin with the biscuit crumb mixture and leave to set in the fridge. Leave for a minimum of 8 hours or, ideally, overnight. Serve straight from the fridge and turn out on to glass plates, remove the clingfilm, and serve with the mango sauce.

5 To make the fresh mango sauce, whizz the mango flesh in the processor with the icing sugar. If need be, thin down with a little water.

TO PREPARE AHEAD Prepare ahead and keep in the fridge for up to 48 hours.

TO FREEZE Freeze in the ramekins.

TO THAW Allow to defrost in the fridge overnight and serve from the fridge so that they are firm.

FRESH SUMMER FRUIT CHEESECAKE V

A wonderful cooked cheesecake. Expect its centre to dip in the middle once cooked, which gives you a space to put lots of fruit in! If liked, you can add 175g (6 oz) sultanas to the cheesecake mixture with the egg whites before baking, and in this case forget the decoration of fresh fruit.

Serves 8–10

BISCUIT BASE
75g (3 oz) digestive biscuits, crushed
40g (1½ oz) butter, melted but not hot
25g (1 oz) demerara sugar

TOPPING
fresh fruit (strawberries, cherries or
   raspberries)
a little redcurrant jelly, melted

CHEESECAKE
50g (2 oz) butter, softened
175g (6 oz) caster sugar
450g (1 lb) curd cheese
25g (1 oz) plain flour
finely grated rind and juice of 1 lemon
3 eggs, separated
150ml (5 fl oz) double cream, lightly
   whipped

1 Lightly grease a 23cm (9 in) loose-bottomed cake tin or spring-form tin, and line with greased greaseproof paper. You do need to line the tin as the mixture is slack when it goes into the tin and may seep through the bottom. Mix together the ingredients for the base, spread over the base of the tin and press down firmly with the back of a spoon.

2 Measure the butter, sugar, curd cheese, flour, lemon rind and juice and the egg yolks into a large bowl. Beat until smooth, then fold in the lightly whipped cream. Whisk the egg whites until stiff then fold into the mixture. Pour on to the crust in the tin.

3 **:** Put in the Roasting Oven on the grid shelf on the floor with the cold plain shelf on the second set of runners. Bake for 20 minutes. (If the top is not pale golden, remove the plain shelf from above and cook for a few more minutes.) Now transfer the very hot plain shelf to the centre of the Simmering Oven and place the cheesecake on top. Bake for a further 20 minutes until set.

:: Bake on the grid shelf on the floor of the Baking Oven for about 20 minutes until pale golden, then transfer to the centre of the Simmering Oven for a further 20 minutes until set.

4 Leave to cool in the tin – it will sink a little – then run a knife around the edge of the tin and lift out. Remove the paper, decorate with fruits and spoon over melted redcurrant jelly to give it a shine. If the redcurrant jelly is a bit thick, add a little water.

TO PREPARE AHEAD The completed cheesecake can be kept covered in the fridge for up to 8 hours.

TO FREEZE If you intend to freeze the baked cheesecake in the tin, first line the tin closely with clingfilm, to prevent the mixture from reacting with the tin. Or wrap the baked, cold cheesecake, without the fruit topping, in clingfilm and put into a freezer container or large freezer bag. Freeze for up to 1 month.

TO THAW Thaw the cheesecake overnight in the fridge. Complete stage 4.

TO COOK IN A CONVENTIONAL OVEN Bake the cheesecake in the oven preheated to 160°C/325°F/Gas mark 3, for about 1 hour or until set. Turn off the oven and leave the cheesecake in the oven for a further hour to cool. Complete as in stage 4.

CRUSHING BISCUITS

To crush digestive biscuits or other biscuits for a cheesecake base, put into a clean poly bag and roll firmly with a rolling pin. Or use a double thickness of poly bags and *stand* on them until crushed! Very quick and easy.

LEMON MERINGUE PIE V

As this is such a family favourite, I have tested two sizes for the Aga. It is such a joy not to have to line the pastry with foil or greaseproof paper and beans to bake blind. Baking on the floor of the Aga oven always ensures a crisp brown crust.

28cm (11 in) pie (serves 10–12)	23cm (9 in) pie (serves 6)
PASTRY	PASTRY
225g (8 oz) plain flour	175g (6 oz) plain flour
25g (1 oz) icing sugar	15g (½ oz) icing sugar
100g (4 oz) butter	75g (3 oz) butter
1 egg yolk	1 egg yolk
about 2 tablespoons water	about 1 tablespoon water
FILLING	FILLING
4 large lemons	2 large lemons
75g (3 oz) cornflour	40g (1½ oz) cornflour
600ml (20 fl oz) water	300ml (10 fl oz) water
4 egg yolks	2 egg yolks
175g (6 oz) caster sugar	75g (3 oz) caster sugar
MERINGUE	MERINGUE
5 egg whites	3 egg whites
225g (8 oz) caster sugar	115g (4½ oz) caster sugar

1 For the pastry, measure the flour and sugar into a bowl and rub in the butter until the mixture resembles fine breadcrumbs. Add the egg yolk and water and work to a firm dough – this may of course be done in the processor. Use to line a loose-bottomed fluted flan tin of the chosen size. Prick the base with a fork and freeze.

2 Stand the frozen flan tin on a baking sheet and slide on to the floor of the Roasting Oven for 10–15 minutes, turning half way through cooking, until a pale golden colour. Carefully lift out of the oven.

3 For the filling, finely grate the rinds from the lemons and squeeze out the juice. Put the rind, juice and cornflour in a small bowl and blend together. Bring the water to the boil, then stir into the cornflour mixture. Return to the pan and heat on the simmering plate, stirring, until you have a thick 'custard'. Mix the egg yolks and sugar together and stir into the custard. Heat on the Boiling Plate, whisking until it bubbles a couple of

times. Remove from the heat. Allow to cool a little then spread into the pastry case.

4 Next make the meringue. Whisk the egg whites until stiff then add the sugar, a little at a time, whisking hard until it has all been added. Pile the meringue on top of the pie, taking care that there are no gaps.

5 Bake on the grid shelf of the Roasting Oven on the third set of runners for about 2–3 minutes until a gentle brown colour, then transfer to the centre of the Simmering Oven for about a further 15 minutes for the 23cm (9 in) pie and 20 minutes for the 28cm (11 in) pie. The meringue should be soft inside and a little crisp on top. Allow to cool until warm, then turn out on to a flat plate.

TO PREPARE AHEAD Make the pastry and line the flan tin ahead. Bake as in stage 2. Cool, cover and leave in a cool place for up to 12 hours until needed.

TO FREEZE Freeze the baked flan case once completely cold, for up to 2 months.

TO THAW Thaw for about 2 hours at room temperature.

TO REHEAT Not suitable.

TO COOK IN A CONVENTIONAL OVEN Bake the pastry blind in the usual way. Reduce the oven to 150°C/300°F/Gas mark 2 then bake the flan, filled with the lemon mixture and topped with meringue, for about 1 hour for the 28cm (11 in) pie, or about 45 minutes for the 23cm (9 in) pie, until the meringue is crisp and pale beige on the outside and soft and marshmallowy underneath.

WONDERFUL APPLE DESSERT CAKE V

I've been doing this special and remarkably easy recipe for years. Many people have asked me how to cook it in the Aga, so here we go. The apples can be windfalls or even shrivelled ones left in the fruit bowl. Serve warm with ice-cream or crème fraîche as a dessert, or with coffee in the morning as one would a Danish pastry, again warm, dusted with icing sugar.

Serves 6

225g (8 oz) self-raising flour
1 level teaspoon baking powder
225g (8 oz) caster sugar
2 eggs
½ teaspoon almond extract

150g (5 oz) butter, melted
350g (12 oz) cooking apples, peeled and
    cored
25g (1 oz) flaked almonds

1 Lightly grease a deep 20cm (8 in) loose-bottomed cake tin.

2 Measure the flour, baking powder, sugar, eggs, almond extract and melted butter into a bowl, mix well until blended, then beat for a minute. Spread half this mixture into the tin. Thickly slice the apples and lay on top of the mixture in the tin, piling mostly towards the centre. Using 2 dessertspoons, roughly spoon the remaining mixture over the apples. This is an awkward thing to do, but just make sure that the mixture covers the centre well as it will spread out in the oven. Sprinkle with the flaked almonds.

3 ⁞ With the grid shelf on the floor of the Roasting Oven and the cold plain shelf on the second set of runners, cook the cake for about 20 minutes or until pale golden brown, watching carefully. Transfer the plain shelf (which is very hot!) to the middle of the Simmering Oven and then lift the cake very carefully on to this and bake for a further 30–40 minutes or until a skewer comes out clean when inserted into the centre of the cake.

⁞⁞ Bake on the grid shelf on the lowest set of runners in the Baking Oven for about 1¼ hours until a skewer comes out clean when inserted into the centre of the cake. If the cake is getting too brown, protect with the cold plain shelf hung above the cake.

TO PREPARE AHEAD Best made to serve warm, but can be made the day before.

TO FREEZE Once cooked and cold, wrap and freeze. Use within 3 months.

TO THAW Thaw for 6 hours if time allows.

TO REHEAT Reheat in the Simmering Oven on a plate, covered with clingfilm for 1½ hours.

TO COOK IN A CONVENTIONAL OVEN Cook in the oven preheated to 160°C/325°F/ Gas mark 3 for 1½ hours until golden and shrinking away from the sides of the tin.

CANTERBURY TART V

This is quite the best apple tart I know. A deep tart shell of crisp, buttery pastry, filled with a magical mixture that is like tarte au citron combined with grated apples. It freezes well too! If you haven't time to arrange the dessert apples on the top, worry not, it will taste the same! This is a slightly updated version of the one I did in my BBC TV series, Mary Berry at Home. You can use bought shortcrust pastry (a 500g/18 oz pack) if short of time.

Serves 10

PASTRY	FILLING
100g (4 oz) butter, cut in cubes	4 eggs
225g (8 oz) plain flour	225g (8 oz) caster sugar
25g (1 oz) icing sugar, sifted	grated rind and juice of 2 lemons
1 egg, beaten	100g (4 oz) butter, melted
	2 large cooking apples, quartered, cored and peeled (about 350g/12 oz prepared weight)
	2 dessert apples, quartered, cored, peeled and thinly sliced
	about 25g (1 oz) demerara sugar

1 If making the pastry by hand, rub the butter into the flour and icing sugar until the mixture resembles breadcrumbs, then stir in the beaten egg and bring together to form a dough. If made in a processor, combine the flour, butter and icing sugar in the bowl then process until the mixture resembles breadcrumbs. Pour in the beaten egg and pulse the blade until the dough starts to form a ball around the central stem. Form the pastry into a smooth ball, put inside a plastic bag and chill in the fridge for 30 minutes. Roll out and line a round flan tin about 28 × 4cm (11 × 1½ in) in the usual way, forming a small lip round the edge. Chill the tin for a further 30 minutes.

2 To prepare the filling, beat the eggs, caster sugar, lemon rind and juice together in a large mixing bowl. Stir in the warm melted butter then coarsely grate the cooking apples directly into the mixture and mix well. Have ready the thinly sliced dessert apples.

3 Remove the tart tin from the fridge and spread the runny lemon mixture in the base. Level the surface with the back of a spoon and arrange the dessert apple slices around the outside edge, neatly overlapping. Sprinkle the apple slices with demerara sugar.

continued overleaf

4 Slide the tart on to the floor of the Roasting Oven and bake for about 10–15 minutes until the pastry is golden brown, then slide in the cold plain shelf on the second set of runners and bake for a further 15–20 minutes until the apple slices are tinged brown. Transfer to the Simmering Oven for a further 10 minutes until the filling is set.

TO PREPARE AHEAD   Line the tart tin with pastry, cover and keep in the fridge for up to 8 hours. Prepare the filling and keep covered in the fridge for up to 4 hours.

TO FREEZE   Line the tart tin base with a circle of Lift-Off paper or non-stick baking paper before the pastry goes in. (This will guard against any acid from the filling reacting with the metal.) Remove the metal collar from the cooled baked tart. Wrap the tart carefully in clingfilm and seal inside a plastic bag. Freeze for up to 1 month.

TO THAW   Thaw for about 8 hours at room temperature.

TO REHEAT   Put back into the metal flan tin. Reheat in the Roasting Oven on the grid shelf on the floor for about 15 minutes.

TO COOK IN A CONVENTIONAL OVEN   Put a heavy baking tray into the oven to preheat, then bake the tart at 200°C/400°F/Gas mark 6, for about 40–50 minutes or until the centre feels firm to the touch and the apple slices are tinged brown.

MENDING CHINA

When I'm mending china, I put it on the back of the Aga, and the glue sets very quickly.

MINCEMEAT AND APPLE CARAMEL

Use dessert or cooking apples, whichever you have to hand. This is the sort of recipe that you can assemble in 10 minutes and cook for Sunday pud! You can use suet-free vegetarian mincemeat if you like.

Serves 8

175g (6 oz) self-raising flour
1 teaspoon baking powder
50g (2 oz) caster sugar
50g (2 oz) soft baking margarine
1 egg
grated rind of 1 lemon
150ml (5 fl oz) milk
225g (8 oz) mincemeat
450g (1 lb) apples, peeled weight, sliced
　　(toss in a little lemon juice if preparing
　　ahead)

TOPPING
50g (2 oz) butter, melted
about 175g (6 oz) demerara sugar

1 Well grease a shallow round 28cm (11 in) ovenproof dish. Measure the flour, baking powder, caster sugar, margarine, egg and lemon rind into a bowl. Beat well together, add the milk and beat again until the consistency of a sponge mixture.

2 Spread the mixture on the base of the dish, spread over the mincemeat and arrange the apple on top. Brush or drizzle butter over the apple and sprinkle with demerara sugar.

3 Place on the grid shelf on the floor of the Roasting Oven and bake for about 25 minutes until the apples are pale golden and the sponge cooked. If the top is getting too brown before the sponge is cooked, slide the cold plain shelf above on the second set of runners.

4 Serve warm with crème fraîche or cream.

TO PREPARE AHEAD Make the sponge mixture and spread it in the dish. Cover with clingfilm and keep in the fridge for up to 8 hours. Prepare the apples and finish the topping just before baking.

TO FREEZE Best not frozen.

TO COOK IN A CONVENTIONAL OVEN Bake in the oven preheated to 230°C/450°F/ Gas mark 8 for about 35 minutes until the top has caramelised to a deep golden brown.

DOUBLE CHOCOLATE PUDDINGS V

This is a wonderful alternative pudding which can be prepared ahead but is best cooked to serve straightaway.

Serves 8

butter

50g (2 oz) cocoa powder, sifted

6 tablespoons boiling water

100ml (4 fl oz) milk

3 eggs

175g (6 oz) self-raising flour

1 rounded teaspoon baking powder

100g (4 oz) soft baking margarine

275g (10 oz) caster sugar

1 × 200g (7 oz) bar of plain chocolate, broken into divided squares

icing sugar for dusting

1 Butter eight size 1 (9cm/3½ in) ramekins and line the bases with buttered greaseproof paper. No need to line the base if you are not turning them out.

2 Put the cocoa in the processor or mixer, set the machine in motion and carefully spoon in the boiling water. Blend for 1–2 minutes then scrape down the sides of the bowl and add the remaining cake ingredients, apart from the chocolate and icing sugar. Process again until the mixture has become a smooth, thickish batter. Divide the mixture between the prepared ramekins, and stack 4 squares of chocolate in the centre of each.

3 **⁞** Bake on the grid shelf on the floor of the Roasting Oven with the cold plain shelf on the second set of runners for 15 minutes, until the top of the pudding is set firm and shrinking away from the sides of the dish.

⁞⁞ Bake on the grid shelf on the floor of the Baking Oven until the top of each pudding is firm and shrinking away from the sides of the dish, about 15 minutes.

4 Serve straight from the oven dusted with icing sugar or allow to settle for 4–5 minutes, turn out and dust with icing sugar. Serve with a little single cream.

TO PREPARE AHEAD Prepare the chocolate puddings to the end of stage 2. Cover and keep in the fridge for up to 24 hours.

TO FREEZE Freeze the raw chocolate mixture in the ramekins for up to 6 weeks.

TO THAW Thaw overnight in the fridge.

TO REHEAT Bake as directed above, allowing 2–3 minutes longer.

TO COOK IN A CONVENTIONAL OVEN Cook at 200°C/400°F/Gas mark 6 for about 15–20 minutes.

ICED LEMON FLUMMERY V

This without doubt is the most asked-for pud from our Aga workshop days. It's fast to make and very refreshing to eat. I think desserts in individual dishes make serving so much simpler. You can keep them in the freezer, then, 10 minutes before serving, take as many as you need out to decorate. They are served still frozen like a sorbet.

Serves 8–12, depending on the size of the ramekins

FLUMMERY

300ml (10 fl oz) double cream
finely grated rind and juice of 2 lemons
350g (12 oz) caster sugar
600ml (20 fl oz) milk

TOPPING

150ml (5 fl oz) whipping cream, whipped
sprigs of fresh mint or lemon balm

1 Pour the double cream into a bowl and whisk until it forms soft peaks. Stir in the lemon rind, juice, sugar and milk and mix well until thoroughly blended.

2 Pour into a shallow 1.5 litre (50 fl oz) plastic container, and cover with a lid. Freeze for at least 6 hours, until very firm.

3 Cut the frozen cream into chunks and process in a processor or blender until smooth and creamy.

4 Pour into individual ramekin dishes, stand the ramekins on a flat large plate or tray, cover with clingfilm and return to the freezer overnight.

5 To serve, spoon a small blob of cream on top of each ramekin and decorate with a sprig of mint or lemon balm.

TO PREPARE AHEAD   Complete to the end of stage 4.

TO FREEZE   Complete stage 4 and freeze for up to a month.

RASPBERRIES WITH MASCARPONE IN A CHOCOLATE CRUST V

A delicious tart to serve on a summer evening, and it can be prepared well in advance.

Serves 8–10

BISCUIT BASE
225g (8 oz) plain chocolate
225g (8 oz) Hobnob biscuits

1 teaspoon vanilla extract
caster sugar to taste (remember the glaze will be sweet)

FILLING
2 × 250g (9 oz) tubs of Mascarpone cheese
1 × 200ml (7 fl oz) carton of full-fat crème fraîche

TOPPING
700g (1½ lb) raspberries
3–4 tablespoons redcurrant jelly

1 Take a 25cm (10 in) spring-release tin and line with a double layer of clingfilm.

2 Melt the chocolate in a medium-sized bowl in the Simmering Oven until just runny and melted. It is even better to do this just standing the bowl on the back of the Aga, where it will take a couple of hours.

3 Coarsely crush the biscuits in a poly bag and add to the warm melted chocolate. When well blended press, using the back of a metal spoon, into the lined tin to about 5cm (2 in) deep around the edge. Make sure that the top edge is neat, and transfer to the fridge to set.

4 Mix the filling ingredients together. Remove the base from the fridge and release the spring-release clip of the tin. Pull the clingfilm to remove the chocolate case from the tin.

5 Put the chocolate biscuit shell on a large plate and remove the metal base. Spread the filling over the chocolate base and cover the filling with the raspberries, rounded side uppermost. Heat the redcurrant jelly carefully on the Simmering Plate, adding water if necessary, and brush over the raspberries. Decorate with raspberry leaves if available. This is easier to cut if served at room temperature.

TO PREPARE AHEAD Make up to 12 hours ahead. Cover and keep in the fridge.

TO FREEZE Not suitable.

TO COOK IN A CONVENTIONAL OVEN Melt the chocolate in a bowl over a pan of gently simmering water.

BAKING IN THE AGA

The Aga might have been invented for those of us who like to bake at home. Four-oven Aga owners would seem to be at an advantage, having the reliable medium heat of the Baking Oven, but all of the cakes in the following chapter can be just as successfully baked in a two-oven Aga. All it requires is an understanding of various Aga techniques.

⁚ *Two-oven Aga* What you do in most cases is put the cake on the grid shelf on the floor of the Roasting Oven with the cold plain shelf above on the second set of runners. Often a cake might be transferred to the Simmering Oven to sit on the by now red-hot plain shelf to finish cooking. (The plain shelf is *invaluable* to Aga bakers.)

⁘ *Four-oven Aga* What you do in most cases is put the cake in the Baking Oven on the grid shelf on the floor for its full cooking time. The cold plain shelf might need to be slid in above the cake towards the end of the cooking time.

Follow the instructions in this chapter to the letter: we have been perfecting these recipes over the years, and they really work.

I described in *The Aga Book* how the Aga cake baker could be used, normally by two-oven Aga owners. Here, though, I've given you recipes that work perfectly without that, admittedly fantastic, piece of equipment. The cakes are baked in round tins of various sizes, in muffin tins and in the large and small roasting tins. I've even cooked some small cakes and muffins directly on the Simmering Plate – the Aga griddle. When making loaf cakes, though, I strongly advise that you make them in two 450g (1 lb) loaf tins rather than one 900g (2 lb) tin, because the latter will go too brown on the outside and will not be properly cooked in the middle.

ENGLISH MUFFINS ^V

These old-fashioned English muffins are traditionally pulled apart, not cut, at the middle, and eaten warm with lashings of butter. Any left over will store for 2–3 days in an airtight container and are then best toasted. If you haven't any semolina, just use flour for dusting.

Makes about 12–14

700g (1½ lb) strong plain flour
1½ level teaspoons caster sugar
1 sachet easy-blend dried yeast

1½ level teaspoons salt
about 450ml (15 fl oz) tepid milk
a little semolina for dusting

1 Measure the dry ingredients into the processor and process for a moment to mix, then switch on again and add the tepid milk in a continuous stream through the feed tube to mix the ingredients to a soft dough, adding a little more milk if need be. Blend for a further 30 seconds to knead the mixture.

2 Turn the dough out on to a surface sprinkled with semolina and roll out to a thickness of about 1cm (½ in) with a rolling pin dusted with semolina.

3 Cut the dough into rounds using a 7.5cm (3 in) plain cutter. Place on a tray dusted with semolina and dust the tops with more semolina. Cover loosely with a large polythene bag, without touching the muffins. (I use a dry cleaning bag and support it with spice jars!) Leave in a warm place until doubled in size, about 1 hour, or in a cool place, 2 hours.

4 Lift the lid of the Simmering Plate to cool a little about 20 minutes ahead. Lightly oil the plate. Cook the muffins in two batches for about 6 minutes on the first side and 8 minutes on the second. When cooked they should be well risen and brown on both sides, and when broken in half the muffin should be done.

5 Cool slightly on a wire rack before splitting and serving with butter and home-made jam. We like them toasted best.

TO PREPARE AHEAD Not suitable.

TO FREEZE Cool, pack and freeze for up to 3 months.

TO THAW Thaw at room temperature for 2–3 hours.

TO REHEAT Best split in half and toasted.

TO COOK IN A CONVENTIONAL OVEN Lightly oil a griddle or heavy-based frying pan. Cook the muffins over a moderate heat on the hob for about 7 minutes on each side until golden and cooked through.

CLASSIC SCOTTISH SHORTBREAD V

We offer these with coffee at Aga workshops. We tried serving other biscuits but everyone insisted that we kept to the shortbread. Take care to cook through the underneath of the shortbread. It should be a very pale biscuit colour and not at all soggy. Using semolina gives a lovely crunch, but if you don't have semolina, use cornflour instead. To make less, halve the ingredients and use a small roasting tin.

Makes 48 triangular biscuits

350g (12 oz) plain flour	TOPPING
175g (6 oz) caster sugar	25g (1 oz) demerara sugar
350g (12 oz) butter, cubed	
175g (6 oz) semolina	

1 Measure the flour, caster sugar, butter and semolina into a processor and process until thoroughly combined. (This can be done by hand, rubbing the butter into the flour first then adding the other ingredients and working together to form a ball.)

2 Press the shortbread mixture into the large roasting tin and level with the back of a spoon so that the mixture is the same depth all the way across. Sprinkle with the demerara sugar.

3 **⦂** Slide the tin on to the lowest set of runners in the Roasting Oven with the plain cold shelf on the second set of runners for about 10 minutes until a pale golden colour (turning round half way through if necessary). Do watch very carefully. Transfer the tin to the Simmering Oven for a further 30–40 minutes until the shortbread is cooked through.

⦂⦂ Bake in the Baking Oven on the lowest set of runners for 10 minutes. Slide in the cold plain shelf on the second set of runners for a further 15 minutes, then transfer to the Simmering Oven for a further 10–15 minutes until cooked.

4 Remove from the oven and allow to cool for a few minutes, then gently cut across by 6 and by 4, and cut each square in half diagonally. Lift out and leave to cool on a cooling rack.

continued overleaf

TO PREPARE AHEAD   Keep the shortbread in an airtight container for up to 1 week.

TO FREEZE   Pack the shortbread into rigid freezerproof containers and freeze for up to 2 months.

TO THAW   Thaw at room temperature for 1–2 hours.

TO COOK IN A CONVENTIONAL OVEN   Bake in the oven preheated to 160°C/325°F/ Gas mark 3, for about 30–40 minutes until pale golden and cooked through. All ovens vary so keep a strict eye on the shortbread.

ST CLEMENT'S SHORTBREAD V

The plain version is always served at our Aga workshops and is so popular we have done this variation from time to time.

Makes 48 triangular biscuits

350g (12 oz) plain flour	TOPPING
100g (4 oz) caster sugar	25g (1 oz) demerara sugar
50g (2 oz) light muscovado sugar	25g (1 oz) flaked almonds
350g (12 oz) butter, cubed	
175g (6 oz) semolina	
grated rind of 1 large orange and	
2 lemons	

1 Measure the flour, sugars, butter, semolina and grated orange and lemon rinds into a processor and process until thoroughly combined. (This can be done by hand, rubbing the butter into the flour first then adding the other ingredients and working together to form a ball.)

2 Press the shortbread mixture into the large roasting tin and level with the back of a spoon so that the mixture is the same depth all the way across. Sprinkle evenly with the demerara sugar and flaked almonds.

3 Bake, cut and cool as for the Classic Scottish Shortbread on page 174. Store or freeze in the same way as well.

ORANGE AND SULTANA SCOTCH PANCAKES V

These are cooked on the Simmering Plate, rather than in an oven, and are delicious for tea.

Makes 8–12

100g (4 oz) self-raising flour	grated rind and juice of 1 small orange
15g (½ oz) soft baking margarine	1 egg
15g (½ oz) caster sugar	about 3 tablespoons milk
75g (3 oz) sultanas	

1 Lift the Simmering Plate lid for about 30 minutes before cooking the pancakes to cool the plate down.

2 Measure all the ingredients into a bowl and beat until smooth. The mixture should be a thickish batter – you may have to add a little more milk.

3 Take a piece of kitchen paper, make it into a pad, then dip in oil and grease the Simmering Plate. Take a tablespoon of the batter, pour on to the Simmering Plate, and spread to a round of about 6.5cm (2½ in). Allow to lightly brown underneath, and let the top set, about 2–3 minutes. Turn over and cook for a further 2 minutes. Lift off and keep warm covered with a tea-towel. Continue cooking until all the batter has been used up.

4 Serve warm with butter. Some might like maple syrup or honey as well.

TO PREPARE AHEAD   These are best freshly made.

TO FREEZE   Not really suitable, as they go rubbery.

TO COOK IN A CONVENTIONAL OVEN   Prepare a griddle or heavy-based frying pan (preferably non-stick) by heating on the hob and lightly greasing with oil. Cook the pancakes on the hot griddle or in the pan for 2–3 minutes, turning once when lightly brown underneath and the top set, and cook for a further 1–2 minutes.

WINTER WELSHCAKES V

Very easy to make from store-cupboard ingredients, and they are wonderful for tea on a cold day. Make when you've had a good cooking session on the Aga and the temperature is down. Traditionally they are served plain with caster sugar, but if liked, can be served with butter and jam.

Makes about 20

350g (12 oz) self-raising flour	100g (4 oz) currants
2 teaspoons baking powder	1 level teaspoon ground mixed spice
175g (6 oz) butter	1 egg
115g (4½ oz) caster sugar	about 2 tablespoons milk

1 Lift the lid of the Simmering Plate to cool the plate for about 15–30 minutes (depending on the heat of your Simmering Plate), before cooking the Welshcakes.

2 Measure the flour and baking powder into a large bowl and rub in the butter until the mixture resembles fine breadcrumbs. Add the sugar, currants and spice. Beat the egg with the milk then add this to the mixture to form a firm dough.

3 Roll out the dough on a lightly floured work surface to a thickness of 5mm (¼ in), and cut into rounds with a 7.5cm (3 in) plain round cutter. Re-roll the trimmings and continue pressing out with the cutter.

4 Grease the Simmering Plate lightly with oil – dip a piece of kitchen paper in the oil – or place an ungreased sheet of Lift-Off paper over it without oiling. Cook the Welshcakes for about 3 minutes on each side until golden brown. (Be careful not to cook the cakes too fast, otherwise the centres will not be fully cooked through.)

5 Cool on a wire rack, then dust with caster sugar. Best eaten on the day of making, preferably warm.

TO PREPARE AHEAD   Measure the ingredients ahead of time, but best baked fresh.

TO FREEZE   Freeze the cooled Welshcakes for up to 6 months.

TO THAW   Thaw for about 2 hours at room temperature.

TO REHEAT   Reheat in the Simmering Oven on a baking tray for about 15 minutes until hot. If necessary, dust again with caster sugar.

TO COOK IN A CONVENTIONAL OVEN   Heat and lightly grease a griddle or heavy-based frying pan (preferably non-stick). Cook the Welshcakes on a low heat for about 3 minutes each side until golden brown and cooked through.

AMERICAN CHOCOLATE MUFFINS V

If you are a real chocoholic you can double up on the chocolate drops! Use plain, milk or white chocolate drops.

Makes 12

225g (8 oz) self-raising flour	100g (4 oz) chocolate drops
1 tsp baking powder	1 egg
25g (1 oz) cocoa powder	175ml (6 fl oz) milk
100g (4 oz) light muscovado sugar	75ml (2½ fl oz) sunflower oil

1 You will need a 12-hole muffin tin, lined with 12 paper muffin cases.

2 Measure all the ingredients into a bowl and beat well. Distribute evenly among the paper cases.

3 Bake on the grid shelf on the floor of the Roasting Oven with the cold plain shelf on the second set of runners for about 15–20 minutes until well risen and cooked through.

TO PREPARE AHEAD Best eaten freshly made.

TO FREEZE Pack and freeze for up to 4 months.

TO THAW Thaw at room temperature for about 2 hours.

TO COOK IN A CONVENTIONAL OVEN Bake in the oven preheated to 200°C/400°F/Gas mark 6 for 20–25 minutes.

BANANA AND WALNUT MUFFINS V

A very good way of using over-ripe bananas. Their flavour is enhanced by the nuttiness of the walnuts.

Makes 12

225g (8 oz) self-raising flour

I tsp baking powder

150g (5 oz) light muscovado sugar

75g (3 oz) shelled walnuts, roughly chopped

3 ripe bananas, mashed with a fork

I egg

175ml (6 fl oz) milk

75ml (2½ fl oz) sunflower oil

icing sugar

1 You will need a 12-hole muffin tin, lined with 12 paper muffin cases.

2 Measure all the ingredients (apart from the icing sugar) into a bowl and beat well. Distribute evenly among the paper cases.

3 Bake on the grid shelf on the floor of the Roasting Oven, with the cold plain shelf on the second set of runners, for about 15–20 minutes until well risen and cooked through.

4 Dust with icing sugar before serving.

TO PREPARE AHEAD Best eaten freshly made.

TO FREEZE Pack and freeze for up to 4 months.

TO THAW Thaw at room temperature for about 2 hours.

TO COOK IN A CONVENTIONAL OVEN Bake in the oven preheated to 200°C/400°F/ Gas mark 6 for 20–25 minutes.

NIC-NOC'S COURGETTE BUNS V

Nicola (Nic-Noc to all of us) was with us for 2 years before she set off on her travels around the world. Nic-Noc first tasted this recipe in Edinburgh at her Grandpa's eightieth birthday weekend. Don't be put off by the courgettes because the buns really do taste good.

This recipe can also be made in 2 × 450g (1 lb) loaf tins. Don't try to do it in one 900g (2 lb) loaf tin as the outside becomes too crusty before the middle is done.

Makes 12

2 eggs
100ml (4 fl oz) sunflower oil
225g (8 oz) caster sugar
150g (5 oz) courgettes, coarsely grated
75g (3 oz) wholemeal self-raising flour
75g (3 oz) self-raising flour

$\frac{1}{2}$ level teaspoon baking powder
$\frac{1}{4}$ teaspoon freshly grated nutmeg
$\frac{1}{4}$ teaspoon ground mixed spice
a little demerara sugar or a few flaked
   almonds to sprinkle if liked

1 Heavily grease a non-stick 12-hole large muffin tin, or line the tin with paper muffin cases instead of greasing.

2 Whisk the eggs, oil, sugar and courgette together using an electric whisk with the beaters on slow speed. Gradually add the remaining ingredients except for the sugar or almonds. Mix to a thickish batter. Divide the mixture between the muffin tins, and sprinkle the top with sugar or almonds if liked.

3 Bake on the grid shelf on the floor of the Roasting Oven with the cold plain shelf on the second set of runners for about 15 minutes, turning half way through. When the buns are cooked they should be golden brown and will spring back when gently pressed with the fingertips.

4 Immediately, carefully remove the buns from the tins and cool on a wire rack.

TO PREPARE AHEAD Best made and eaten on the day they are baked.

TO FREEZE Wrap and freeze, for up to 2 months.

TO THAW Thaw at room temperature for about 4 hours.

TO COOK IN A CONVENTIONAL OVEN Bake in the oven preheated to 200°C/400°F/ Gas mark 6 for about 20 minutes.

MINCEMEAT CAKE

An all-the-year-round cake that I've made for years. As I've said before, loaf tins of 450g (1 lb) cook best in the Aga, so you will make two here. I usually serve one for tea then put the second one in the freezer for another day. Even loaf tins this size vary; I use a pair from Lakeland Limited that work perfectly. You could use vegetarian mincemeat, without the suet.

Makes 2 loaf cakes

2 eggs	100g (4 oz) currants
150g (5 oz) caster sugar	225g (8 oz) self-raising flour
150g (5 oz) soft margarine	a few flaked almonds
225g (8 oz) mincemeat	

1 Line and grease two 450g (1 lb) loaf tins (top measurement 17 × 11cm/6½ × 4 in).

2 Crack the eggs into a large bowl and add the other ingredients except the flaked almonds. Mix well until blended, then divide the mixture between the two tins and level out evenly. Sprinkle with flaked almonds.

3 ⦂ Put the tins on the grill rack in the lowest position in the large roasting tin. Bake in the Roasting Oven on the lowest set of runners with the cold plain shelf two sets of runners above for about 25 minutes until golden brown. Transfer the roasting tin and loaf tins to the middle of the Simmering Oven for about 35 minutes or until the cakes are golden, firm to the touch, and an inserted skewer comes out clean.

⦂⦂ Put the grid shelf on the floor of the Baking Oven, and bake the loaves one behind the other for about 40–45 minutes. When a perfect golden brown (after about 25 minutes) you may need to slide the cold sheet on to the second set of runners. The cakes are done when a skewer inserted into the centre comes out clean.

4 Allow the cakes to cool in the tins for a few minutes, then loosen the sides with a small palette knife, turn out on to a wire rack and leave to cool.

TO PREPARE AHEAD The cakes will keep for up to 1 week, wrapped and stored in an airtight container.

TO FREEZE Wrap the cakes and freeze for up to 2 months.

TO THAW Thaw for about 4 hours at room temperature.

TO COOK IN A CONVENTIONAL OVEN Bake in the oven preheated to 160°C/325°F/ Gas mark 3 for about 1¼ hours, or until the cakes are golden brown, firm to the touch and a skewer inserted into the centre comes out clean.

TOO-GOOD-TO-MISS CARROT TRAYBAKE V

Not just carrots, but bananas and walnuts as well! Double the recipe and it will of course cook perfectly in the large roasting tin. This will take about 10 minutes longer to cook.

Cuts into about 15 pieces

225g (8 oz) self-raising flour

2 level teaspoons baking powder

150g (5 oz) light muscovado sugar

100g (4 oz) carrots, coarsely grated

2 ripe bananas, mashed

2 eggs

150ml (5 fl oz) sunflower oil

50g (2 oz) shelled walnuts, chopped

TOPPING

225g (8 oz) Philadelphia Light cream cheese

75g (3 oz) butter, softened

175g (6 oz) icing sugar, sifted

a little vanilla extract

1 Line the small roasting tin with foil and grease it well. Measure all the traybake ingredients except the walnuts into a bowl. Beat well with a wooden spoon or with an electric beater until smooth, then fold in the nuts. Pour into the tin.

2 Bake on the grid shelf on the floor of the Roasting Oven, with the cold plain shelf on the second set of runners above, for about 30–40 minutes, turning once after 25 minutes. Cook until pale golden and shrinking away from the sides of the tin.

Bake on the grid shelf on the floor of the Baking Oven for about 30–40 minutes, until pale golden and shrinking away from the sides of the tin. If the top is getting too brown after 25 minutes, slide the cold plain shelf above on the second set of runners.

3 Cool. Turn out on to a tray or board and remove the foil.

4 Measure the ingredients for the topping into a mixer, and mix until smooth. Spread over the cake, swirling with a spatula. Chill before serving, cut into pieces.

TO PREPARE AHEAD   Weigh out ingredients earlier in the day, and line the tin.

TO FREEZE   Leave whole, un-iced, wrap in foil and freeze for up to 2 months.

TO THAW   Thaw for about 6 hours at room temperature, then ice it, and cut up.

TO COOK IN A CONVENTIONAL OVEN   Bake in the oven preheated to 180°C/350°F/ Gas mark 4 for about 45–50 minutes, until the cake is well risen, golden brown and firm to touch. Make the icing as in stage 5.

A wonderful spread for tea, with a Whole Orange Spice Cake *(see page 188)* as well as Too-Good-to-Miss Carrot Traybake.

LEMON YOGHURT CAKE V

A really moist plain cake which is best eaten within the week. Like a Madeira cake, it doesn't need icing. This amount of mixture fills 2 × 450g (1 lb) loaf tins. Don't attempt to cook it in one large 900g (2 lb) loaf tin as it is apt to burn, being in the oven for a longer time.

Makes 2 loaf cakes

75g (3 oz) butter, softened	1 × 200g (7 oz) carton of Total Greek
300g (11 oz) caster sugar	yoghurt
3 eggs, separated	225g (8 oz) self-raising flour
grated rind of 1 lemon	

1 Grease and line two 450g (1 lb) loaf tins (top measurement 17 × 11 cm/6½ × 4 in) with a long strip of greased greaseproof paper to also go up two of the sides of the tin.

2 Measure the butter and sugar into a bowl, and cream together using a hand-held electric whisk until thoroughly blended. Add the egg yolks and grated lemon rind, blend well, then add the yoghurt. Mix until smooth, then fold in the flour.

3 Whisk the egg whites with an electric whisk until stiff but not dry, and fold into the cake mixture. Divide the mixture between the two tins, and gently level the surface.

4 ⦂ Bake on the grid shelf on the floor of the Roasting Oven with the cold plain shelf on the second set of runners for about 35 minutes. If the cakes are becoming too dark cover loosely with foil.

⦂⦂ Bake on the grid shelf on the floor of the Baking Oven for about 35 minutes.

5 To test whether done, insert a skewer. When it comes out clean with no uncooked mixture sticking to it, it is done. Turn the cakes out and allow to cool.

TO PREPARE AHEAD The cakes will keep for up to a week, stored in an airtight container in a cool place.

TO FREEZE Wrap and freeze the cake at the end of stage 5 for up to 2 months.

TO THAW Thaw for about 4 hours at room temperature.

TO COOK IN A CONVENTIONAL OVEN Bake in the oven preheated to 180°C/350°F/ Gas mark 4 for 45–50 minutes or until the cakes are well risen, golden and firm to the touch.

TREACLE SPICE TRAYBAKE V

Don't be too worried if the traybake dips in the centre – it means you were a little generous with the treacle. To make it easy, warm the treacle on the back of the Aga and weigh on top of the sugar in the scale pan, adding the two weights together.

Makes 15–20 slices

225g (8 oz) soft baking margarine
175g (6 oz) caster sugar
225g (8 oz) black treacle
300g (11 oz) self-raising flour
2 teaspoons baking powder
1 teaspoon ground mixed spice
1 teaspoon ground allspice
4 eggs
4 tablespoons milk
3 bulbs stem ginger from a jar, finely
  chopped

ICING
75g (3 oz) icing sugar, sieved
about 2 tablespoons stem ginger syrup
  from the jar
2 bulbs stem ginger, finely chopped

1 Measure all the ingredients for the cake into a large bowl and beat well for about 2 minutes until well blended. Line a small roasting tin about 30 x 23 cm (12 x 9 in) with foil and grease well.

2 ⦂ Hang on the lowest set of runners of the Roasting Oven with the plain cold shelf on the second set of runners and cook for 20–25 minutes until deep brown and set round the edges. Transfer the hot plain shelf to the centre of the Simmering Oven and slide the roasting tin on top of it. Allow to cook for 15–20 minutes until cooked.

⦂⦂ Bake on the grid shelf on the floor of the Baking Oven for about 35–45 minutes. Should it be getting a little too dark at the edges, slide the plain cold shelf on to the second set of runners to slow down the cooking.

3 Remove from the oven and allow to cool.

4 To make the icing, mix together the icing sugar and syrup, pour over the cake and sprinkle with the chopped stem ginger. If preferred, dust with sifted icing sugar.

TO FREEZE Leave whole, un-iced, wrap in foil and freeze for up to 2 months.

TO THAW Thaw for about 6 hours at room temperature, then ice and cut into 15–20 squares.

TO COOK IN A CONVENTIONAL OVEN Cook in a preheated oven at 180°C/350°F/ Gas mark 4 for about 40 minutes. Cool and ice as above.

WHOLE ORANGE SPICE CAKE V

A fresh, spiced orange cake. If liked, you can ice the cake as well as fill it. Use just under half the orange filling to sandwich the cakes together, and spread the rest on top.

Serves 8

1 small thin-skinned orange	ORANGE FILLING
275g (10 oz) self-raising flour	2 level tablespoons orange pulp,
3 level teaspoons baking powder	reserved from above
275g (10 oz) caster sugar	50g (2 oz) soft butter
225g (8 oz) soft baking margarine	175g (6 oz) icing sugar, sieved, plus a
4 eggs	little extra for dusting
1 teaspoon ground cinnamon	
1 teaspoon mixed spice	

1 Grease and base line two deep 20cm (8 in) tins with greased greaseproof paper.

2 Place the whole orange in a small saucepan, cover with boiling water and cook in the Simmering Oven until soft, about 1½ hours.

3 When the orange is soft and cold, cut in half and remove any pips. Process the whole orange, including the skin, until medium chunky. Reserve 2 level tablespoons of the orange pulp for the icing, and put the rest back in the processor. Add the remaining cake ingredients and blend until smooth. Avoid over-mixing. Divide the mixture evenly between the two tins.

4 ⦙ Bake on the grid shelf on the floor of the Roasting Oven with the cold plain shelf on the second set of runners for about 20–25 minutes, turning after 15 minutes. When the cakes are cooked, they should be shrinking away from the sides of the tins, and be pale golden brown.

⦙⦙ Bake on the grid shelf on the floor of the Baking Oven for about 20–25 minutes, turning after 15 minutes. When the cakes are cooked, they should be shrinking away from the sides of the tins, and be pale golden brown.

5 Leave to cool in the tins for a few moments, then turn out, peel off the paper, and finish cooling on a wire rack.

6 To make the orange filling, cream the soft butter, then add the sieved icing sugar and reserved orange pulp. Sandwich the cakes together with the icing, and sift icing sugar over the top of the cake.

TO PREPARE AHEAD   Best eaten freshly made, but it will store in an airtight container for 2–3 days.

TO FREEZE   Pack and freeze the filled cake for up to 2 months.

TO THAW   Thaw for about 2–3 hours at room temperature.

TO COOK IN A CONVENTIONAL OVEN   Cook the orange in water on the hob very slowly until completely tender, about an hour. Bake the cake at 180°C/350°F/Gas mark 4 for about 25–30 minutes. Fill and ice as above.

ORANGES

Thin-skinned oranges are usually smaller – avoid using Jaffa oranges as they have a very thick pith.

BUTTER ALMOND CAKE **V**

This makes two 450g (1 lb) loaf cakes, one for now and one for the freezer. It is essential to have the butter at a soft creamy stage, not oily. I usually do this by standing the mixing bowl containing the butter on a tea-towel at the back of the Aga.

Makes 2 loaf cakes

175g (6 oz) butter, softened
175g (6 oz) caster sugar
4 eggs
100g (4 oz) ground almonds
200g (7 oz) self-raising flour
2 level teaspoons baking powder
2 tablespoons milk
$\frac{1}{4}$–$\frac{1}{2}$ teaspoon almond extract

TOPPING
about 25g (1 oz) flaked almonds

1 Grease and line two 450g (1 lb) loaf tins with greased greaseproof paper.

2 Measure the softened butter and all the other cake ingredients into a bowl and beat until smooth. Turn into the prepared tins. Sprinkle with flaked almonds. Stand the tins on the grill rack in the lowest position in the large roasting tin.

3 ⁚ Slide on to the lowest set of runners in the Roasting Oven with the cold plain shelf on the second set of runners. Bake for about 45 minutes, turning half way through if necessary, until pale golden and a skewer comes out clean when inserted.

⁙ Slide on to the lowest set of runners in the Baking Oven and bake for about 45 minutes until pale golden and a skewer comes out clean when inserted. Check half way through cooking. If the cakes are too brown, slide in the cold plain shelf on the second set of runners.

4 Cool in the tins before removing. Serve warm or cold.

TO PREPARE AHEAD   Just weigh out the ingredients and cover, up to a day ahead.

TO FREEZE   Cool the cooked cake(s), put into a polythene bag, and freeze for up to 6 months.

TO THAW   Thaw at room temperature for 4 hours.

TO COOK IN A CONVENTIONAL OVEN   Bake in the oven preheated to 180°C/350°F/ Gas mark 4 for about 45 minutes. Cover with foil if getting too brown.

BANANA BUTTER CAKE V

This mixture makes two fairly shallow loaf cakes. It is very similar to the Butter Almond Cake opposite, but with the flavour of bananas instead of almonds.

Makes 2 loaf cakes

4 medium bananas, mashed	100g (4 oz) butter, softened
250g (9 oz) self-raising flour	200g (7 oz) caster sugar
2 level teaspoons baking powder	2 eggs

1 Grease and line two 450g (1 lb) loaf tins with greased greaseproof paper.

2 Measure all the ingredients into a bowl and beat until smooth. Spoon half of the mixture into each tin. Stand the tins on the grill rack in the lowest position in the large roasting tin.

3 Bake as for the two- and four-oven Agas in the Butter Almond Cake recipe opposite. Cool and serve warm or cold.

TO PREPARE AHEAD   Follow preparation and freezing notes as for Butter Almond Cake (opposite).

BANANAS

This is an excellent way of using slightly over-ripe bananas – the ones that sit in the fruit bowl and everyone avoids!

AMERICAN LIGHT CHRISTMAS CAKE V

This is a little tricky to bake, but just watch the colour carefully and you will be amply rewarded. It is very, very important to drain and dry the fruit well. If they are at all wet, the cake may become mouldy.

Makes 1 cake

350g (12 oz) glacé cherries	75g (3 oz) ground almonds
1 × 200g (7 oz) can of pineapple in natural juice	5 eggs
350g (12 oz) no-soak dried apricots	TO DECORATE
100g (4 oz) whole almonds	whole almonds, blanched
finely grated rind of 2 lemons	glacé cherries, halved
350g (12 oz) sultanas	
250g (9 oz) self-raising flour	TO FINISH (OPTIONAL)
250g (9 oz) caster sugar	100g (4 oz) icing sugar, sifted
250g (9 oz) soft baking margarine	

1 Grease a 23cm (9 in) deep round cake tin, and line the base and sides with a double layer of greased greaseproof paper.

2 Cut each cherry into quarters, rinse and drain well. Drain and roughly chop the pineapple, then dry both the cherries and pineapple very thoroughly on absorbent kitchen paper. Snip the apricots into pieces. Blanch the whole almonds in boiling water, then skin and roughly chop. Place the prepared fruit and nuts in a large washing-up or mixing bowl with the grated lemon rind and sultanas and gently mix. Add the remaining ingredients and beat well for 1 minute until smooth. Turn the mixture into the prepared cake tin. Level the surface and decorate the top with blanched whole almonds and halved glacé cherries.

3 ⁝ Stand a grill rack in its lowest position in the large roasting tin, and place the cake on top. Slide the roasting tin on to the lowest set of runners in the Roasting Oven, with the cold plain shelf above on the second set of runners. Bake the cake for about 30 minutes until a pale golden brown – the colour of a perfect Victoria sandwich. Watch very carefully. Then transfer roasting tin and cake to the Simmering Oven and cook for about a further 2½ hours until a skewer comes out clean when inserted into the cake.

⁝⁝ Cook on the grid shelf on the lowest set of runners in the Baking Oven for 1 hour, sliding the cold plain shelf on to the set of runners above if the cake is getting too brown. Watch very carefully. Transfer to the Simmering Oven for a further 45–60 minutes until a skewer comes out clean when inserted into the cake.

4 Leave to cool in the tin for about 30 minutes, then turn out and cool completely on a wire rack.

5 You can glaze the cake if liked. Mix the sieved icing sugar with enough water to give a thin icing, and drizzle over the top of the cake.

TO PREPARE AHEAD Ideally, this cake should be made 1 month ahead and kept in the larder, covered with foil.

TO FREEZE This freezes well, for up to 2 months.

TO THAW Thaw at room temperature for 12 hours.

TO COOK IN A CONVENTIONAL OVEN Cook in the oven preheated to 160°C/325°F/ Gas mark 3 for about 2¼ hours until golden brown. Insert a skewer to test – if it comes out clean, the cake is cooked. It may be necessary after 1 hour to cover it loosely in foil to prevent it from getting too brown.

FLOWER STEMS

If you have flowers such as Christmas roses that need their stems sealed, instead of burning the stems or dipping them in boiling water, put them straight down on the Boiling Plate of the Aga.

NORFOLK FRUIT CAKE WITH GINGER V

This cake is really moist, and packed with fruits, including apricots and cherries. It is a good fruit cake even without the ginger. Simply increase the other fruits to make up the weight if you have no ginger in the store-cupboard. If you have an Aga cake baker, you could use it. Remember to preheat it on the floor of the Roasting Oven (see The Aga Book). It will take about 1¼ hours.

Makes 1 cake

450g (1 lb) mixed fruits and nuts, such as apricots, roughly chopped; cherries, quartered; shelled nuts, roughly chopped; raisins, sultanas	225ml (8 fl oz) water
	2 eggs, beaten
	275g (10 oz) self-raising wholemeal flour
100g (4 oz) butter or margarine	2 teaspoons ground ginger
1 teaspoon bicarbonate of soda	100–175 (4–6 oz) stem ginger, drained
175g (6 oz) light muscovado sugar	of syrup, roughly chopped

1 Grease and line a 20cm (8 in) deep round cake tin.

2 Measure the prepared fruits and nuts, butter or margarine, bicarbonate of soda, sugar and water into a large pan. Bring up to the boil on the Boiling Plate, and boil for 3 minutes.

3 Allow to cool, then add the eggs, flour, ground ginger and stem ginger. Mix to thoroughly combine then turn into the prepared cake tin and level the top.

4 **:** Stand the cake tin in the large roasting tin on the grid rack in the lowest position and hang on the lowest set of runners in the Roasting Oven, with the cold plain shelf on the second set of runners from the top. Cook for 30 minutes. If after 20 minutes it is getting a little brown at the sides, give it a gentle half turn. Transfer the now hot plain shelf to the centre of the Simmering Oven, lift the cake carefully on top of it, and cook for a further 1–1½ hours.

:: Put the cake on the grid shelf on the floor of the Baking Oven for about 1¼ hours. Check after 30 minutes, and if the top is getting too brown, slide the cold plain shelf on the second set of runners from above to prevent it from browning more.

5 Cool in the tin before turning out on to a cooling rack.

TO PREPARE AHEAD This cake keeps well as it is so moist. Cool completely, then wrap in greaseproof paper and foil and store in a cool place for up to 2 months.

TO FREEZE Wrap the cake in clingfilm, then put into a large freezer bag, and freeze for up to 3 months.

TO THAW   Remove the wrappings and thaw for about 8 hours at room temperature.

TO COOK IN A CONVENTIONAL OVEN   Bake in the oven preheated to 160°C/325°F/ Gas mark 3 for about 1¼–1½ hours or until a skewer inserted into the centre comes out clean, and the cake is firm to the touch.

CRUNCHY ICED LEMON TRAYBAKE V

Make this in the small roasting tin lined with foil, or double the recipe for the large roasting tin (bake this for about 30–35 minutes). It is delicious served warm or cold. When we were in Australia we had a similar cake with poppy seeds (about 40g/1½ oz added to the sponge mixture). It was always served warm, heated in a microwave: I would do this in the Simmering Oven.

Cuts into about 24 pieces

225g (8 oz) self-raising flour
225g (8 oz) caster sugar
3 eggs
175g (6 oz) soft baking margarine
1½ level teaspoons baking powder
finely grated rind of 2 lemons
6 tablespoons milk

TOPPING
175g (6 oz) granulated sugar
juice of 2 lemons

1 Line the small roasting tin with foil, and grease well with extra margarine or butter.

2 Measure all of the cake ingredients into an electric mixer or bowl and beat well until smooth. Turn the mixture into the lined tin.

3 ⁞ Hang the small roasting tin on the lowest set of runners in the Roasting Oven and slide the cold plain shelf on the second set of runners. Bake for about 25 minutes or until the cake is golden brown and coming away from the sides of the tin. Turn the tin round after 20 minutes if the baking is not even.

⁞⁞ Hang the roasting tin on the lowest set of runners in the Baking Oven. Should the cake become too brown after, say, 20 minutes, slide the cold plain shelf above the traybake on the second set of runners.

4 Remove cake from the oven. Mix together the topping ingredients and pour over the surface of the hot cake. Leave the cake in the tin until barely warm, then use the foil lining to lift the cake out. Cut into about 24 pieces.

TO PREPARE AHEAD Best freshly made, although it will keep in an airtight container for a few days.

TO FREEZE Freeze whole well wrapped in foil for about 2 months.

TO THAW Thaw at room temperature for 2–3 hours.

TO COOK IN A CONVENTIONAL OVEN Bake in the oven preheated to 180°C/350°F/ Gas mark 4 for 30–35 minutes.

WICKED CHOCOLATE BROWNIES V

These are expensive to make, but worth it, and are even better when kept for a couple of days. As with all chocolate brownies, expect the mixture to sink slightly after baking.

Makes about 32 pieces

275g (10 oz) soft baking margarine	75g (3 oz) cocoa powder
375g (13 oz) caster sugar	100g (4 oz) plain flour
4 eggs	1 × 100g (4 oz) packet of plain chocolate
1 teaspoon baking powder	'polka dots'

1 Line the small roasting tin with foil and grease well.

2 Put all the ingredients together into a bowl and mix until well blended. This can be done in a processor, mixing in the 'polka dots' by hand at the last minute. Spoon the mixture into the roasting tin and level the top.

3 ⦂ Put the tin on the grid shelf on the floor of the Roasting Oven with the cold plain shelf above on the second set of runners, and bake for about 25 minutes until set. Then very carefully transfer the now-hot plain shelf to the middle of the Simmering Oven and bake the brownies on it for about a further 20 minutes, or until a skewer comes out clean when inserted into the centre of the cake. Expect a slight dip in the centre when baked.

⦂⦂ Put the grid shelf on the floor of the Baking Oven, and bake the brownie mixture for about 25 minutes, making sure that the top does not get too dark. If it does, slip the cold plain shelf above on the second set of runners for the last 5 minutes. Then transfer the roasting tin to the centre of the Simmering Oven for a further 20 minutes or so, until a skewer comes out clean when inserted into the centre of the cake.

4 Cool in the tin. Remove the foil and cake from the tin. Store wrapped in more foil, or in a cake tin in the larder. Cut into squares to serve.

TO PREPARE AHEAD   Make ahead, cool, cut into squares and keep in an airtight container for up to 1 week.

TO FREEZE   Pack and freeze the cake whole when completely cold, for up to 6 months.

TO THAW   Thaw at room temperature for 2–3 hours.

TO COOK IN A CONVENTIONAL OVEN   Cook in the oven preheated to 190°C/375°F/ Gas mark 5 for about 40–45 minutes.

BLACK OLIVE AND CHEESE BREAD V

This can be made in a processor if preferred. Measure the dry ingredients into the processor, then pour liquid down the funnel and process until the dough leaves the side of the processor bowl – about 1–2 minutes. The recipe can also be used to make rolls, see opposite.

Makes 2 loaves

700g (1½ lb) strong white flour
2 teaspoons salt
1 packet fast-action dried yeast
(McDougalls)
450ml (15 fl oz) warm water (150ml/
5 fl oz boiling + 300ml/10 fl oz cold)
3 tablespoons good olive oil

50g (2 oz) stoned black olives, ideally in
oil, drained and chopped
40g (1½ oz) Parmesan, grated
40g (1½ oz) mature Cheddar, grated
freshly ground black pepper
beaten egg to glaze

1 Measure the flour into a large bowl, and add the salt and yeast. Add the warm water and oil, and mix to a pliable dough. You may need a little more water – I always find that it is better to have a slightly sticky dough than a dry one.

2 Turn the dough on to a floured table and knead for 5 minutes. Return the dough to the bowl, cover with clingfilm and stand on a wire rack by the Aga. Leave for about 1½ hours until doubled in size.

3 Take the dough out of the bowl, and knock back by kneading for a few minutes. Flatten out a little and work in the olives, half the cheeses and a little pepper.

4 Divide the dough in half, then shape each piece into a smooth round and place on a large greased baking sheet or on Lift-Off paper. Brush with egg and sprinkle with the remaining grated cheeses.

5 Cover the tray with a large polythene bag and leave to rise for about 30 minutes until the loaves have doubled in size.

6 Bake in the Roasting Oven on the grid shelf on the floor for about 20–25 minutes, until the bread is golden and sounds hollow when tapped on the base. If the top is getting too brown, slide in the cold plain shelf above on the second set of runners. Eat warm or leave to go cold.

7 To make rolls, at stage 4, divide the dough into 24 pieces and roll into balls. Place on two greased baking sheets or Lift-Off paper. Glaze and prove as before. Bake in the Roasting Oven on the grid shelf on the floor for about 15 minutes. If the bases of the rolls are not quite brown, place the baking sheet directly on the floor of the Roasting Oven for a further 5 minutes.

TO PREPARE AHEAD   Weigh up ingredients earlier in the day.

TO FREEZE   Cool the baked bread quickly, then seal in freezer bags, label and freeze for up to 6 months.

TO THAW   Thaw the bread in the freezer bag for 5–6 hours at room temperature.

TO REHEAT   Remove from freezer bag. Refresh and reheat in the middle of the Simmering Oven for about 20 minutes.

TO COOK IN A CONVENTIONAL OVEN   Bake the bread at 230°C/450°F/Gas mark 8 for 10 minutes, then lower the temperature to 200°C/400°F/Gas mark 6 for a further 20–25 minutes, until golden and the base sounds hollow when tapped.

BREAD MAKING

When you leave bread to rise, always cover it well to prevent a skin forming on the surface. Use a lightly oiled poly bag or oiled cling film, or a large, oiled, plastic ice-cream container with a lid does the job perfectly.

GRUYÈRE AND SPINACH TART

This has been a great favourite at Aga workshops. The greatest joy is that with an Aga there is no need to bake the pastry blind first. You can make your own pastry as below, or use a bought 500g (18 oz) packet of shortcrust pastry.

Serves 8

PASTRY	FILLING
225g (8 oz) plain flour	350g (12 oz) lean bacon pieces, chopped
100g (4 oz) butter	1 large onion, chopped
1 egg yolk	350g (12 oz) young fresh spinach,
2–3 tablespoons water to mix	shredded, or 450g (1 lb) frozen leaf
	spinach, thawed and really well drained
	5 eggs and 1 egg white (just 5 eggs if
	using bought pastry)
	300ml (10 fl oz) double cream
	300ml (10 fl oz) milk
	salt and freshly ground black pepper
	175g (6 oz) Gruyère or Emmental
	cheese, grated

1 First make the pastry. Measure the flour into a bowl and rub in the butter until the mixture resembles fine breadcrumbs. Mix to a dough with the egg yolk and the water – all this can be done in a processor. Work together. Chill for half an hour or so in the fridge.

2 Roll the pastry out on a lightly floured surface. Use to line a large, deepish, oval flan dish 33 × 25cm (13 × 10 in), or a 28–30.5cm (11–12 in) deepish, round flan dish. Flute the top edge. Chill until ready to cook.

3 Put the bacon pieces in a large non-stick frying pan on the Simmering Plate and allow the fat to run out. Add the onion, transfer to the Boiling Plate to brown for a few moments, then transfer to the floor of the Simmering Oven for 15 minutes or so until the onion is tender. Return to the Boiling Plate, add the spinach, and stir-fry for a couple of minutes.

4 Whisk the eggs, cream, milk and seasoning (go easy on the salt if the bacon is salty). Scatter the bacon, onion and spinach over the base of the pastry case, sprinkle over half of the Gruyère cheese, pour over the egg mixture and sprinkle with the remaining cheese.

5 Cook on the floor of the Roasting Oven for about 25–30 minutes, turning after 15 minutes, until the pastry is pale golden brown and the filling is just set and golden all over. If the top is becoming too brown, slide in the cold plain shelf on the second set of runners. Don't be tempted to cook for too long as the filling will puff up and over-cook.

TO PREPARE AHEAD   A day ahead, make the pastry, line the dish, cover with clingfilm and keep in the fridge.

TO FREEZE   Cool and pack after stage 5, for 2 months.

TO THAW   Defrost for about 5 hours at room temperature.

TO REHEAT   Slide directly on to the floor of the Roasting Oven for about 10 minutes.

TO COOK IN A CONVENTIONAL OVEN   Bake the pastry blind in the usual way. Bake the filled tart at 180°C/350°F/Gas mark 4 for about 35–40 minutes, until the filling is set and golden.

CLEANING PANS AND DISHES

To clean encrusted pans and dishes, put some biological clothes washing powder in a sink of hot water. Dissolve it thoroughly by whisking it around with a rubber-gloved hand – otherwise neat powder pits pans. When dissolved, soak your pans and dishes overnight, and any grease will come off easily the next day.

FOOD FOR A CROWD

When you have an Aga, you can happily and confidently cook for a crowd, and it's one of my favourite ways of entertaining. I love the planning, the shopping, the cooking in advance and the final knitting together of all the various strands.

The majority of the recipes here are for ten people, but they can be doubled to serve more if you are organising a really big party. Most of them are capable of being eaten with a fork only, a necessity at a buffet party. Almost all can be cooked in advance, both the main courses and puddings, which leaves you free to concentrate on other party details on the day itself. In fact some of them *must* be cooked the day before – the ham, say, and the poultry for the curry. Be careful, though, to cool bulk-cooked foods quickly: a good tip to speed this process up is to divide a stew or something similar between two smaller dishes before cooling and putting in the fridge.

Puddings are always popular at larger parties, and I have given you some really special dishes here, including my current favourite, The Ultimate Chocolate Roulade. There are a few tarts here, which I think cook to perfection in the Aga, and are very useful because they cut into so many portions. Offer a fruit salad as well, or some ice-cream – and don't forget to look at the Puddings chapter for further inspiration.

CELERY BEEF WITH SUN-DRIED TOMATOES

Great for shoot lunches or as part of a winter buffet, this casserole is given a wonderfully pungent flavour by the sun-dried tomatoes. If from a jar, use a little of the oil to brown the meat.

Serves 10–12

2 tablespoons olive oil	350ml (12 fl oz) beef stock
1.4kg (3 lb) good stewing beef	1 large onion, sliced
2 fat cloves garlic, crushed	12 sun-dried tomatoes, coarsely
50g (2 oz) plain flour	chopped
salt and freshly ground black pepper	1 whole head of celery
1½ teaspoons dried basil	2 generous tablespoons redcurrant jelly
350ml (12 fl oz) red wine	1 large red pepper, seeded and cut into
5 tablespoons tomato purée	thin strips

1 Measure the oil into a large non-stick pan on the Boiling Plate, then brown the beef, in batches if necessary. Add the garlic and cook for a further 2 or 3 minutes, stirring well but do not brown the garlic. Sprinkle in the flour and seasoning, stir well and add the basil, wine, tomato purée and finally stock. Bring to the boil, then add the onion and tomatoes.

2 Chop the celery diagonally and add about two-thirds to the casserole, reserving the heart to add later. Stir in the redcurrant jelly.

3 Cover the pan and simmer for 5 minutes, then transfer to the floor of the Simmering Oven, and cook for 2–2½ hours, or until the beef is tender.

4 Just before serving, stir in the reserved chopped celery heart and the red pepper, and cook gently for about 5 minutes. Serve with a herby mash, and vegetables.

TO PREPARE AHEAD Quickly cool at the end of stage 3. Chill for up to 2 days.

TO FREEZE Pack the cold casserole, completed to the end of stage 3, into a freezerproof container and freeze for up to 3 months.

TO THAW Thaw overnight in the fridge.

TO REHEAT Bring up to the boil in an ovenproof casserole dish on the Boiling Plate, stir, then transfer to the Roasting Oven on the second set of runners and reheat for about 20 minutes, until piping hot. Stir in the reserved celery and the red pepper.

TO COOK IN A CONVENTIONAL OVEN Cook in the oven, preheated to 160°C/325°F/ Gas mark 3 for about 2 hours, then add the celery and red pepper.

SPICED TREACLE GAMMON

Choose smoked or unsmoked gammon, on or off the bone, whichever appeals to you most. Once gammon is cooked, it is called ham – confusing! Cooking the gammon overnight means that the Aga is free during the day to do other cooking. In my Aga the gammon is tender after 13 hours so I start cooking it at about 8.30 pm after I've taken whatever is in the Simmering Oven out for supper. The gammon is cooked by about 9.30 the next morning, and just needs skinning and browning. It is sensible to use a meat thermometer to check when the ham is done.

Serves up to 18

a whole gammon, about 7.3kg (16 lb)	English mustard powder
black treacle	demerara sugar
25g (1 oz) black peppercorns, crushed	

1 Soak the gammon in plenty of cold water for 24 hours.

2 Take a large piece of foil – twice the size of the large roasting tin. Line the tin with it, letting the foil overlap. Lift the gammon on top and spread with black treacle. Sprinkle with crushed peppercorns and loosely fold the foil over the top. Slide the roasting tin on to the floor of the Simmering Oven. Cook overnight, for about 14 hours (maybe longer in a slow, older Aga). Check first thing in the morning.

3 Open the foil, pierce the gammon with a skewer in the thickest part and if the skewer goes in easily and the juices that flow out are clear, it is done. If the centre feels firm and the juices are pink, cook for longer. Or you can test the meat with a meat thermometer.

4 Remove the foil, throw away the salty juices and peel off the skin of the gammon when cool enough to handle. Score the fat diagonally with a sharp knife and stand the gammon on a new piece of foil in the roasting tin. Sprinkle with mustard powder and demerara sugar. Slide on the lowest set of runners in the Roasting Oven. Roast until brown, about 20 minutes, serve hot, or allow to cool.

5 If serving cold, chill in the fridge for 12 hours or so, before carving and serving.

continued overleaf

TO PREPARE AHEAD   Cool quickly after cooking, wrap loosely in foil and keep for up to 1 week in the fridge.

TO FREEZE   Not suitable.

TO COOK IN A CONVENTIONAL OVEN   Cook in the oven preheated to 160°C/325°F/ Gas mark 3 for 20 minutes per 450g (1 lb). A meat thermometer should register 75°C/170°F. To glaze, increase the temperature of the oven to 230°C/450°F/ Gas mark 8 for 15–20 minutes until golden.

MEAT THERMOMETERS

With an Aga, a meat thermometer is a great asset, and they are not expensive to buy from good kitchen stores. Put into the thickest part of the meat, not touching the bone, and the thermometer will register the internal heat.

EASTERN CURRY WITH FRUITS

A great hot party dish and very easy. If you like a really spicy flavour add an extra teaspoon of curry powder. We serve this hot but it could be served cold, without heating in the oven just before serving.

Serves 10–12

900g (2 lb) cooked chicken or turkey	2 good tablespoons medium curry powder
10 spring onions	1 × 600g (1 lb 5 oz) jar of thick low-
2 perfect ripe avocados	calorie mayonnaise
2 mangoes	1 × 360g (12 oz) jar of mango chutney,
4 bananas, slightly under-ripe	large pieces cut up
juice of 2–3 lemons, according to size	salt and freshly ground black pepper
50g (2 oz) butter	paprika

1 Cut the meat into practical sized cubes, removing any skin and bone. Chop the spring onions, keeping the white and green part in separate piles. Peel, stone and slice the avocados and mangoes, diagonally slice the peeled bananas, and toss all the fruit in the juice of the lemons. All these want to be in fairly chunky pieces.

2 Melt the butter in a pan on the Boiling Plate and fry the white part of the spring onions until tender. Add the curry powder, allow to cook for a few minutes, and then mix with the mayonnaise and the chutney in a large bowl.

3 Mix all the fruits, lemon juice and chicken or turkey with the mayonnaise mixture, and check the seasoning. Add the green part of the spring onion and pile into a shallow ovenproof dish about 30 × 38cm (12 × 15 in). Sprinkle with paprika.

4 Just before serving, bake in the centre of the Roasting Oven for about 12–15 minutes, watching carefully, until piping hot. Do not allow to over-cook or the mayonnaise will separate. Serve with rice and a green salad.

TO PREPARE AHEAD   Combine the chicken or turkey with the mayonnaise mixture and the green parts of the spring onions up to a day ahead. Cover and keep in the fridge. Cut the avocados, mangoes and bananas just before cooking. Toss in the lemon juice and add to the mixture.

TO FREEZE   Not suitable, as it would separate on thawing.

TO COOK IN A CONVENTIONAL OVEN   Cook in the oven preheated to 220°C/425°F/ Gas mark 7 for about 20–25 minutes until hot through. Be careful not to over-cook or the mayonnaise will separate.

ITALIAN GARDEN LASAGNE V

It is important to season this vegetarian lasagne, with its abundance of mushrooms and tomatoes, very well. The lasagne pasta available now is mostly the dry pre-cooked variety that you don't have to cook to soften first.

Serves 10–12

about 3 tablespoons olive oil

1½ large onions, chopped

700g (1½ lb) button mushrooms, sliced

3 fat cloves garlic, crushed

40g (1½ oz) plain flour

3 × 400g (14 oz) tins of chopped tomatoes

1½ teaspoons dried basil

salt and freshly ground black pepper

1½ teaspoons caster sugar

700g (1½ lb) frozen whole-leaf spinach, thawed and drained

about 225g (8 oz) pre-cooked lasagne

SAUCE

1.3 litres (45 fl oz) milk

1 bay leaf

a few black peppercorns

175g (6 oz) butter

115g (4½ oz) plain flour

generous 1½ teaspoons Dijon mustard

TO FINISH

350g (12 oz) mature Cheddar, grated

1 First infuse the milk for the sauce. Measure the milk into a pan, add the bay leaf and peppercorns, and bring slowly up to just below boiling point on the Simmering Plate. Cover and allow to infuse in the Simmering Oven for about 30 minutes.

2 Heat the oil in a large non-stick frying pan on the Boiling Plate, fry the onion, then add the mushrooms and garlic. Allow to cook for a few minutes, then sprinkle with the flour and blend in. Mix in the tomatoes, basil, salt, pepper and sugar, and bring to the boil, stirring for a couple of minutes. Remove from the heat.

3 Now make the béchamel sauce. Melt the butter in a pan on the Simmering Plate, add the flour, and stir in, then gradually blend in the strained, infused hot milk. Bring to the boil, stirring all the time until thickened. Season with salt, pepper and mustard.

4 Spread one-third of the tomato and mushroom mixture across the base of a shallow ovenproof dish, about 38 × 30cm (15 × 12 in). Make sure that the spinach is really well drained through a colander or sieve. Season with salt and pepper. Use about a third of the spinach dotted in small rounds over the top. Cover with a third of the sauce and a little grated cheese. Lay half the sheets of pasta across the dish and continue to layer up as before, starting with the tomato mixture, then the rest of the pasta and layer again, finishing with the sauce and cheese.

5 Cook in the Roasting Oven on the grid shelf on the floor for about 35–40 minutes until the pasta is cooked and golden brown on top. If browning too much, slide in the cold plain shelf on the second set of runners.

6 Serve with a green salad and French bread or garlic bread if they are a hungry crowd.

TO PREPARE AHEAD   Cool the lasagne at the end of stage 4, cover with clingfilm and keep in the fridge for up to 24 hours.

TO FREEZE   Completely cool, then cover and freeze at the end of stage 4 for up to 3 months.

TO THAW   Thaw at room temperature for 12 hours, then cook as directed in stage 5.

TO COOK IN A CONVENTIONAL OVEN   Cook the lasagne in the oven preheated to 200°C/400°F/Gas mark 6, for 35–40 minutes or until the pasta is cooked and the lasagne golden and bubbling.

EASY ENTERTAINING

When entertaining, and you're short of time (or money), never be afraid to serve the simplest food. So long as it is cooked properly, and is of the best quality, it will be appreciated. A salad can be served as a starter instead of accompanying the main course, and a couple of good cheeses or a bowl of fresh fruit can be the perfect end to a meal.

BEEF FLORENTINE WITH THREE CHEESES

This is well-flavoured minced beef topped with spinach and cheese, then finished with a layer of crisp filo pastry. The sheets of filo that we buy in the local supermarket are Cypressa.

Serves 12

SAVOURY BEEF LAYER

a good knob of butter

1.8 kg (4 lb) good-quality lean minced
    beef

3 level tablespoons plain flour

2 × 400g (14 oz) tins of chopped
    tomatoes

4 fat cloves garlic, crushed

4 good tablespoons tomato purée

1 generous teaspoon caster sugar

salt and freshly ground black pepper

SPINACH AND CHEESE LAYER

450g (1 lb) frozen leaf spinach, thawed

175g (6 oz) mature Cheddar, grated

175g (6 oz) Gruyère or Emmental
    cheese, grated

225g (8 oz) rich cream cheese

4 eggs, beaten

TOPPING

about 17 sheets filo pastry

melted butter for brushing

1 First cook the minced beef. Melt the butter in a large pan on the Simmering Plate, add the meat and cook, stirring. When the natural fat begins to run out, transfer to the Boiling Plate and brown the meat. Add the flour, mix well, then add the tomatoes, garlic, tomato purée, sugar and seasoning. Bring to the boil, simmer for 5 minutes, cover and transfer to the Simmering Oven. Bake for 45 minutes until tender. Check the seasoning.

2 Next mix the spinach filling. Squeeze all of the water out of the spinach. Turn into a bowl with the cheeses, then add the eggs, season with salt and pepper and mix well.

3 Spread half of the beef mixture in a shallow ovenproof dish, about 38 × 30cm (15 × 12 in). Top with the spinach mixture, then with a layer of the remaining beef.

4 Spread about 5 sheets of the filo pastry out on a table. Brush with melted butter. Cover the surface of the beef with 3 layers of filo, using the 5 buttered sheets of filo, trimming to fit. Brush the remaining 12 sheets with butter. Scrunch up each sheet and arrange on top of the layered filo. This means that each person gets a crispy piece of filo, and the dish is easier to cut into portions.

5 Bake on the grid shelf on the floor of the Roasting Oven for about 30–35 minutes until golden brown and bubbling at the edges.

TO PREPARE AHEAD   Prepare to the end of stage 3. Cover with a large polythene bag or foil and keep in the fridge for up to 24 hours.

TO FREEZE   Freeze at the end of stage 3 for up to 1 month.

TO THAW   Thaw for about 8 hours at room temperature. Proceed from stage 4.

TO COOK IN A CONVENTIONAL OVEN   Cook in the oven preheated to 220°C/425°F/ Gas mark 7 for 30–35 minutes, until piping hot and the pastry is golden brown.

FREEZING SENSE

Freeze the cooked beef and spinach layers in an ovenproof dish that will also go in the freezer. When frozen, the block can be transferred to a poly bag, and the dish released for another use. When you want to thaw and reheat, transfer the frozen block from the bag back to the same dish.

CHEESE AND ROCKET TART WITH PARMESAN PASTRY V

The tart case here is made of a wonderful thin cheese pastry, and the filling is a classic onion and cheese mixture, with the addition of the salad leaf of the moment, rocket. You can use a 500g (18 oz) packet of bought shortcrust pastry if time is short.

Serves 10

PARMESAN PASTRY	FILLING
225g (8 oz) plain flour	2 tablespoons olive oil
¼ teaspoon salt	2 large Spanish onions, finely sliced
1 teaspoon English mustard powder	2 cloves garlic, crushed
100g (4 oz) butter, cut into small pieces	225g (8 oz) Gruyère cheese, grated
75g (3 oz) Parmesan, grated	100g (4 oz), fresh rocket
1 large egg, beaten	4 eggs
	600ml (20 fl oz) single cream
	salt and freshly ground black pepper

1 First make the pastry. Measure the flour, salt, mustard and butter into the processor or a bowl, and process or rub in until the mixture resembles fine breadcrumbs. Add the Parmesan and the beaten egg and mix again just as long as it takes for the ingredients to come together. Chill for 30 minutes wrapped in clingfilm.

2 Heat the oil in a large non-stick frying pan and cook the onion on the Boiling Plate for a few minutes. Cover, transfer to the Simmering Oven, and leave for 15–20 minutes until soft. Return to the Boiling Plate with the garlic for a few minutes to caramelise. Cool.

3 Roll the pastry thinly on a lightly floured work surface and use to line a 28cm (11 in) deep, loose-bottomed, round flan tin. Chill if time allows.

4 Spoon the cooled onion into the flan case, then add the grated cheese and roughly chopped rocket. Beat the eggs and add the cream and seasoning. Pour into the flan case.

5 Cook on the floor of the Roasting Oven for about 20 minutes, until the pastry is brown, then put on the grid shelf on the floor of the Roasting Oven for a further 10 or 15 minutes until the filling is just set and golden all over. If the top is becoming too brown, slide in the cold plain shelf on the second set of runners.

continued overleaf

TO PREPARE AHEAD   Make the pastry and line the flan tin. Cover with clingfilm and keep in the fridge for up to a day ahead.

TO FREEZE   Cool, pack and freeze at the end of stage 5 for up to 1 month.

TO THAW   Thaw for about 5 hours at room temperature.

TO REHEAT   Reheat on the grid shelf on the floor of the Roasting Oven for about 15 minutes.

TO COOK IN A CONVENTIONAL OVEN   Bake the pastry blind in the usual way. Bake the filled tart in the oven, preheated to 180°C/350°F/Gas mark 4 for about 35–40 minutes, until the filling is set and golden.

CELEBRATION CHICKEN

This is easy and particularly suitable for the Aga as it is cooked in the ovens. If you are weight-watching, substitute half the cream with stock and thicken with a level tablespoon of cornflour blended with a little cold stock.

Serves 10

2 large onions, finely sliced	10 chicken breasts, skin on
65g (2½ oz) butter	600ml (20 fl oz) pouring double cream
salt and freshly ground black pepper	3 tablespoons chopped parsley
2 tablespoons sweet, mild paprika	

1 Cook the onion in 15g (½ oz) of the butter in a large non-stick frying pan on the Boiling Plate for a few minutes. Cover and transfer to the floor of the Simmering Oven for about 20 minutes, or until soft.

2 Melt the remaining butter on the Boiling Plate, transfer to a large bowl, and add salt, pepper and paprika. Dip the skin side of each chicken breast into the mixture. Well butter the large roasting tin, sprinkle with salt and pepper, then arrange the chicken inside, skin side up.

3 Slide the roasting tin on to the top set of runners in the Roasting Oven and roast the chicken breasts for 15 minutes or until just cooked.

4 Spread the cooked onion over the base of a large oval or oblong shallow ovenproof dish, and season. Arrange the chicken on top, cover with foil and put in the Simmering Oven for a few minutes while the sauce is made.

5 First check that there is no fat left in the roasting tin. If there is, just mop it up with a little kitchen paper. Deglaze the roasting tin with the cream. Slide the tin on to the floor of the Roasting Oven for a few minutes, and allow to just bubble up and boil – watch carefully. Check the seasoning and pour over the chicken and onions. Sprinkle with parsley and serve.

TO PREPARE AHEAD   Make the dish to the end of stage 5, omitting the parsley. Cool, cover and keep in the fridge for up to 24 hours.

TO FREEZE   Freeze at the end of stage 5, again without the parsley, for up to 2 months.

TO THAW   Thaw for about 6 hours at room temperature or overnight in the fridge.

TO REHEAT   Reheat on the grid shelf on the floor of the Roasting Oven for about 15–20 minutes until piping hot. Sprinkle with fresh parsley to serve.

TO COOK IN A CONVENTIONAL OVEN   Cook the onion and brown the chicken breasts on top of the hob. Make the sauce, pour over the chicken and cook in the oven, preheated to 200°C/400°F/Gas mark 6 for about 15–20 minutes until cooked through and piping hot.

A TROUBLE-FREE PARTY

The secret is to plan well in advance. Select recipes that need a minimum of last-minute preparation – guests have come to see and talk to *you*, and you shouldn't be in the kitchen all the time. And also choose dishes that will not spoil if kept waiting, either by late guests, or by that absorbing conversation over drinks.

BAKED PENNE WITH
BACON AND MUSHROOMS

This is one of the most popular lunch dishes we serve at Aga workshops. For every day, omit the cream and top with just 225g (8 oz) grated, well-flavoured Cheddar. Prepare the topping just before baking. If you have difficulty in getting chestnut mushrooms, use small ordinary mushrooms.

Serves 10

salt and freshly ground black pepper

350g (12 oz) onions, roughly chopped

225g (8 oz) dried penne (quills)

700g (1½ lb) dry-cured streaky bacon, sliced and cut up small

25g (1 oz) butter

450g (1 lb) small chestnut mushrooms, sliced

450g (1 lb) frozen whole-leaf spinach, thawed and really well drained

SAUCE

1.6 litres (55 fl oz) milk

a few black peppercorns

a few bay leaves

100g (4 oz) butter

75g (3 oz) plain flour

1 teaspoon Dijon mustard

2 tablespoons lemon juice

FINAL TOPPING

150ml (5 fl oz) pouring double cream

40g (1½ oz) Parmesan, grated

50g (2 oz) Mozzarella cheese, grated

1 First infuse the milk for the sauce. Put the milk, peppercorns and bay leaves into a pan. Bring to just below boiling point on the Simmering Plate, cover and transfer to the Simmering Oven for about 1 hour if time allows.

2 Just under half fill a large pan with water, add 1 tablespoon salt, bring to the boil on the Boiling Plate, and add the onion and pasta. Bring back to the boil, stirring. Simmer for about 10 minutes until al dente. Rinse in a colander with lots of cold water.

3 Spread the bacon out in the roasting tin, and cook in the Roasting Oven, tossing from time to time, until crisp. Drain off any fat during cooking and keep.

4 Melt half the butter in a large pan on the Boiling Plate, add any bacon fat and stir-fry the mushrooms quickly. Season and add to the bacon.

5 Next make the sauce. Melt the butter on the Boiling Plate, add the flour and cook for a few minutes. Strain off the infused milk and gradually add to the roux. Allow to thicken to a thin sauce, stirring continuously. Add the mustard and lemon juice, and season. Cool then stir in the onion, pasta, bacon and mushrooms. Pour into an ovenproof oblong dish, about 38×30cm (15×12 in).

6 Melt the remaining butter on the Simmering Plate, and toss the spinach in this. Season well. Put 10 piles of spinach into the dish, push down into the pasta and level a bit.

7 Just before cooking, season the cream, pour over the dish and sprinkle with the cheeses.

8 Place the dish on the grid shelf near to the top of the Roasting Oven, and cook for about 30 minutes until hot right through, with a crispy top.

9 When serving, try to give each person a portion of spinach with the pasta. Serve with a green or tomato salad. Garlic bread or warm rolls can be served too, if people are hungry.

TO PREPARE AHEAD   Prepare up to a day ahead up to the end of stage 5. Cover with clingfilm and keep in the fridge.

TO FREEZE   Freeze at the end of stage 5 for up to 1 month.

TO THAW   Thaw overnight or about 12 hours at room temperature.

TO REHEAT   Proceed from stage 6.

TO COOK IN A CONVENTIONAL OVEN   Cook in the oven preheated to 200°C/400°F/ Gas mark 6 for about 30–35 minutes until hot right through with a crispy top. Reheating from cold will take slightly longer.

SMOKED HADDOCK FLORENTINE

This very easy version of a fish pie is made in a large dish, and it's great for kitchen supper for a crowd. Ideally assemble the pie the day before. Coating the haddock in cornflour prevents the sauce from becoming too wet. You could serve the pie with rice or mashed potato, but more often than not I just serve garlic or herb bread.

Serves 10

a generous knob of butter	BÉCHAMEL SAUCE
450g (1 lb) button mushrooms, thickly sliced	1.2 litres (40 fl oz) milk
700g (1½ lb) fresh young spinach	1 onion, peeled and halved
salt and freshly ground black pepper	1 bay leaf
freshly grated nutmeg	a few parsley stalks
6 hard-boiled eggs, shelled and sliced	100g (4 oz) butter
1.1kg (2½ lb) undyed smoked haddock fillet, skinned and coated in about 40g (1½ oz) seasoned cornflour	100g (4 oz) plain flour
	100g (4 oz) mature Cheddar, grated
	2 teaspoons Dijon mustard
40g (1½ oz) fresh breadcrumbs	
75g (3 oz) Parmesan, freshly grated	

1 Measure the milk for the sauce into a saucepan, and add the onion halves, bay leaf and parsley stalks. Bring to just under boiling point on the Boiling Plate, cover and transfer to the Simmering Oven for 30 minutes to flavour the milk. Season with salt and pepper.

2 Melt the butter for the sauce on the Simmering Plate in a roomy pan, then pull the pan aside from the heat and stir in the flour. Gradually add the strained, infused hot milk, return the pan to the heat and slowly bring to the boil, stirring continually until thickened. Cover the pan with a lid to prevent a skin forming.

3 Melt the knob of butter in a large, deep frying pan and fry the mushrooms briskly for a minute or two. Add the spinach to the mushrooms and cook gently until it has just wilted. Drain the spinach and mushrooms and season well with salt, pepper and nutmeg.

4 Mix 6 tablespoons of the béchamel sauce with the spinach and mushrooms and spread on the base of a shallow, buttered ovenproof dish, about 38 × 30cm (15 × 12 in). Cover the spinach and mushrooms with sliced hard-boiled eggs.

5 Cut the haddock into manageable-sized pieces to give two small pieces per person. Sit these pieces on top of the eggs.

continued overleaf

6 Add the grated Cheddar and Dijon mustard to the remaining sauce and pour over the raw fish. Sprinkle the top with mixed breadcrumbs and Parmesan.

7 Bake the haddock for about 30 minutes on the second set of runners in the Roasting Oven until the haddock is cooked and the topping is golden brown.

TO PREPARE AHEAD   Complete to the end of stage 6, cover with clingfilm and keep in the fridge for up to 24 hours.

TO FREEZE   Can be frozen, without the hard-boiled eggs, for up to 1 month.

TO THAW   Thaw for about 6 hours at room temperature or overnight in the fridge.

TO COOK IN A CONVENTIONAL OVEN   Cook in a preheated oven at 220°C/425°F/ Gas mark 7 for about 35 minutes.

DEFROSTING FISH

I defrost the fish my son often catches, by leaving them in their polythene wrapping, covered with an old towel, and putting them in a dish in the Simmering Oven.

BAKED MARINATED FRESH SALMON

This is a very easy way to prepare a whole salmon, and it's a very stylish presentation too. The sauce is very simple yet delicious. A good fishmonger or fish department in a supermarket will happily fillet and skin one side of the fish.

Serves 10–12

1 × 2.7kg (6 lb) salmon, filleted, one fillet only skinned, yielding about 1.6kg (3½ lb) weight	SAUCE
juice and grated rind of 2 limes	1 × 425g (15 oz) tin of lobster or crab bisque
4 tablespoons chopped fresh dill	juice of 1 small lemon
salt and freshly ground black pepper	4 tablespoons pouring double cream
25g (1 oz) butter	1 tablespoon chopped fresh dill
1 large onion, finely chopped	
450g (1 lb) fresh baby spinach	
freshly grated nutmeg	

1 Put the salmon fillets into a large shallow, non-metallic dish. Pour over the lime juice, grated rind and the chopped dill. Season, cover and marinate in the fridge overnight.

2 Melt the butter in a large non-stick frying pan on the Boiling Plate, add the onion, and cook for a few minutes. Cover and transfer to the floor of the Simmering Oven until almost transparent, about 15 minutes. Return to the Boiling Plate, and add the spinach – it looks too much at first but will cook down a lot. Stir continuously until all the moisture has evaporated. Season with salt, pepper and freshly grated nutmeg. Allow the filling to cool.

3 Well butter a large sheet of foil, and lay the skinned salmon fillet, skinned side down, on the foil. Season the fish, and spread the spinach mixture evenly over the surface. Put the second side of salmon, skin side down on a chopping board. Cut through the flesh, but *not* through the skin, into ten to twelve portions, allowing larger portions at the tail and smaller portions as the salmon widens. Season the fish and place it 'cut' side down, skin side up, on to the spinach.

4 Lift the foil over and secure tightly at the ends and side. The salmon is now loosely wrapped in a secure parcel like a giant Cornish pasty. Leave in the fridge until required.

continued overleaf

5 Put on a baking sheet, skin side upwards, and slide on to the grid shelf on the floor of the Roasting Oven for 30 minutes, turning the baking sheet round once during this time. To test for doneness, carefully open the foil and check that the salmon has changed to an opaque pink. It will then be done.

6 When ready to serve, lift the salmon from the foil on to a long plate and carefully peel the skin off the top. Dust with chopped parsley. The salmon will easily cut into neat slices.

7 For the sauce, heat the can of bisque on the Boiling Plate, stir in the lemon juice and cream, and bring up to boiling point. Season with salt, pepper and chopped dill. Serve with the salmon.

TO PREPARE AHEAD   Prepare the salmon to the end of stage 4 and keep in the fridge for up to 24 hours.

TO FREEZE   Not suitable.

TO COOK IN A CONVENTIONAL OVEN   Cook in the oven preheated to 200°C/400°F/ Gas mark 6 for about 25–30 minutes until the salmon is an opaque pink.

SKINNING FISH

If you have to skin the fish yourself, put some salt on your fingers – to prevent the fish from slipping – and hold the fish by the tail. Using a sharp knife, skin from tail to head with quick, short, sawing strokes, keeping the edge of the blade close to the surface of the skin so that no flesh is lost.

CHICKEN BREASTS WITH ORANGE AND BASIL

An unusual but delightful flavour combination. If you have no chicken stock to hand, use a cube.

Serves 12

salt and freshly ground black pepper

12 chicken breasts, boned and skinned

8 tablespoons extra-thick-cut marmalade, chopped

a good handful of fresh basil leaves, finely chopped (leave a few whole for garnish)

6 cloves garlic, crushed

grated rind and juice of 2 oranges (keep separate)

about 50g (2 oz) butter, softened

4 teaspoons cornflour

900ml (30 fl oz) chicken stock

1 Sprinkle the base of the large roasting tin with some seasoning and arrange the chicken breasts on top.

2 Combine the marmalade, chopped basil, crushed garlic, orange rind and butter in a bowl with some additional seasoning. Mix well and spread the mixture over the chicken.

3 Slide on to the top set of runners in the Roasting Oven and roast for about 15 minutes, basting once or twice with the pan juices. Test to make sure the chicken is cooked, then remove from the roasting tin to a warmed serving dish. Cover and keep warm while making the sauce.

4 Skim any fat from the pan juices by tilting the pan so the liquid flows to a corner. Use a tablespoon to take off the surface fat. Mix the fresh orange juice with the cornflour. Pour the stock and orange juice mixture into the roasting tin, combine together with the juices in the pan and blend well. Put on to the floor of the Roasting Oven for a few minutes to boil then remove and whisk corners. Simmer and taste and check seasoning, adding perhaps a dash of sugar if needed.

5 Sprinkle in the reserved basil leaves, torn into shreds, at the very last minute so that they stay bright green. Pour the sauce over the chicken breasts and serve immediately. The amount of sauce is generous so you might like to serve some separately.

TO PREPARE AHEAD   The chicken breasts can be spread with the butter mixture, covered loosely with foil and kept in the fridge for up to 12 hours. Bring up to room temperature before cooking.

TO FREEZE   Cool the cooked chicken quickly, then pack into a freezer container. Freeze the sauce separately. Freeze for up to 3 months.

TO THAW   Thaw for about 4 hours at room temperature.

TO REHEAT   Arrange the chicken breasts in the small roasting tin. Slide into the centre of the Roasting Oven and reheat for about 8 minutes until piping hot. Heat the sauce through on the Boiling Plate.

TO COOK IN A CONVENTIONAL OVEN   Cook the chicken in the oven preheated to 190°C/375°F/Gas mark 5 for about 25–30 minutes, until the chicken is cooked through. Make the sauce on the hob in the usual way.

CHICKEN STOCK

The Aga is perfect for making chicken stock. Raw bones are best, but you can also use the stripped carcasses of roast birds. Pack the carcasses in poly bags and store in the freezer until you have two or three. Then break up the frozen bones with a rolling pin and make stock in the usual way. Because the bones are smaller, they take up less room in the pan, and make a more concentrated stock.

PEAR FRANGIPANE TART V

This is a great tart to serve for a party. Always serve it warm. You could use a bought 500g (18 oz) pack of shortcrust pastry if time is short.

Serves 10–12

PASTRY

100g (4 oz) butter, cubed
225g (8 oz) plain flour
25g (1 oz) icing sugar, sifted
1 egg, beaten

FILLING

175g (6 oz) soft butter
175g (6 oz) caster sugar
3 eggs, beaten
175g (6 oz) ground almonds
40g (1½ oz) plain flour
1 teaspoon almond extract
8 fresh, ripe Williams pears, peeled,
    cored and halved
apricot jam, melted and sieved for glaze
25g (1 oz) flaked almonds, toasted

1 If making the pastry by hand, rub the butter into the flour and icing sugar until the mixture resembles breadcrumbs, then stir in the beaten egg and bring together to form a dough. If making in a processor, combine the butter, flour and icing sugar in the bowl then process until the mixture resembles ground almonds. Pour in the beaten egg and pulse the blade until the dough starts to form a ball around the central stem. Form the pastry into a smooth flat cake, wrap in clingfilm and chill for 30 minutes or until manageable.

2 Make the filling in the unwashed processor. Cream the butter and sugar together, then gradually add the beaten eggs (do not worry if it looks curdled at this stage). Scrape down the sides of the bowl with a spatula. Add the ground almonds, flour and almond extract. Process for a few seconds until well incorporated. Leave this mixture in the fridge until required.

3 Roll out the chilled pastry on a lightly floured work surface and line a flan tin 28cm (11 in) in diameter, about 2.5cm (1 in) deep. If possible, chill for a further 30 minutes.

4 Spoon the frangipane mixture into the pastry case and level the top using a small palette knife. Arrange the pear halves, cut side down, attractively on the filling. Be sure to leave enough room between them to allow the frangipane mixture to rise.

5 ⁂ Lift the tin on to a baking sheet and bake on the floor of the Roasting Oven for 15–20 minutes until pale golden. After this time put the cold plain shelf on the second set of runners and continue to bake for a further 15–20 minutes until the almond filling is set and golden brown. If the pastry is becoming too dark, place a ring of foil around the edge.

⁑ Lift the tin on to a baking sheet and bake on the floor of the Roasting Oven until pale golden, about 15–20 minutes. Then, transfer to the centre of the Baking Oven until set and golden brown, another 15–20 minutes.

6 Cool slightly, brush with hot apricot glaze and sprinkle with toasted flaked almonds. Serve warm with cream or crème fraîche.

TO PREPARE AHEAD   The pastry-lined flan tin can be kept, covered with clingfilm, in the fridge for up to 24 hours. Filled with the frangipane mixture it can be kept for about 1 hour, covered and refrigerated.

TO FREEZE   Complete the tart to the end of stage 5, cool, wrap and freeze for up to 1 month.

TO THAW   Thaw the tart for about 8 hours at room temperature.

TO REHEAT   Loosely cover the tart with foil and reheat in the Roasting Oven on the grid shelf on the floor for about 15 minutes.

TO COOK IN A CONVENTIONAL OVEN   Put a heavy flat baking tray into the oven to preheat. Place the tart on the tray and bake at 190°C/375°F/Gas mark 5 for about 45–50 minutes until the almond filling and pastry are golden brown. Complete stage 6 as directed.

DIFFICULTY WITH PASTRY CASES?

If you are in a hurry, sometimes the pastry cracks and the mixture inside runs through the pastry and base of the loose-bottomed flan tin. The solution is to use a ceramic flan dish, cook on the floor of the Roasting Oven all the time to get a brown crisp base, and serve in the dish.

THE ULTIMATE CHOCOLATE ROULADE V

Big, classic and brilliant! Using 10 eggs gives you a massive chocolate roulade, perfect for special occasions. To make it even more special, stir 2 tablespoons of brandy into the whipped cream.

Serves 8–10

275g (10 oz) plain chocolate	TO FINISH
275g (10 oz) caster sugar	450ml (15 fl oz) double cream
10 eggs, separated	icing sugar

1 Grease and line the large roasting tin with non-stick baking paper. Break the chocolate into small pieces into a bowl and stand the bowl on the back of the Aga until the chocolate melts. Cool slightly.

2 Measure the sugar and egg yolks into a large bowl and whisk with an electric whisk on a high speed until light and creamy. Add the cooled chocolate and stir until evenly blended.

3 In a separate bowl, whisk the egg whites until stiff but not dry. Carefully fold into the chocolate mixture. Turn into the prepared roasting tin and gently level the surface.

4 **⦂** Hang the roasting tin on the lowest set of runners in the Roasting Oven and slide the cold plain shelf above on the second set of runners. Bake for about 25 minutes, turning after 18 minutes.

⦂⦂ Hang the roasting tin on the lowest set of runners of the Baking Oven, and bake for about 25 minutes, turning after 18 minutes. If during cooking the roulade looks as though it is browning too quickly, slide the cold plain shelf on the second set of runners above the roulade.

5 The roulade when baked should be firm to the touch and may be slightly dipped in the centre. Remove the cake from the oven, leave in the tin and place a cooling rack over the top of the cake. Place a damp tea towel on top of the rack and leave until cool.

6 Whip the cream until it just holds its shape and dust a large piece of greaseproof paper with sifted icing sugar. Turn out the roulade and peel off the paper. Spread with the cream. Roll up like a Swiss roll, after scoring a mark 2.5cm (1 in) in along the long edge. Roll up very tightly using the paper to help. Do not worry when the roulade cracks – a good one should!

7 Dust with more sifted icing sugar to serve.

continued overleaf

TO PREPARE AHEAD   Complete the roulade to the end of stage 6, up to 24 hours ahead, covered and kept in the fridge.

TO FREEZE   Wrap and freeze the roulade at the end of stage 6, for up to 1 month.

TO THAW   Thaw overnight in the fridge. Unwrap the roulade, transfer to a serving plate and dust with more icing sugar to serve.

TO COOK IN A CONVENTIONAL OVEN   Bake the roulade in a large Swiss roll tin/roasting tin in the centre of the oven, preheated to 180°C/350°F/Gas mark 4, for 25 minutes, or until firm to the touch. Continue as directed.

HAZELNUT MERINGUE TORTE FILLED WITH RASPBERRIES AND CREAM V

I am particularly fond of this meringue. If you have difficulty buying flaked hazelnuts, slice whole hazelnuts on a fine slicing disc in a processor. These, folded into the meringue, give it a delightful flavour and crisp texture. So much better than ground hazelnuts, which are often dry.

Serves 12

MERINGUE	FILLING
6 egg whites	300ml (10 fl oz) whipping cream
375g (13 oz) caster sugar	225g (8 oz) raspberries
1 teaspoon cornflour, slaked with 1 teaspoon white wine vinegar	
175g (6 oz) flaked hazelnuts	

1 Draw two circles on separate sheets of silicone paper (or Lift-Off paper in chalk), one of them 25cm (10 in) in diameter and the other 28cm (11 in) in diameter. Turn over and place on two separate baking trays.

2 Preferably using an electric mixer, whisk the egg whites, on full speed, in a large bowl until stiff but not dry. Still whisking at full speed, gradually add the sugar a teaspoon at a time. The process may take about 8 minutes, depending on the power of the machine. When all the sugar has been added the mixture will be shiny and very stiff. Fold in the vinegar and cornflour, and 150g (5 oz) of the nuts.

3 Use 2 tablespoons to shape about half of the meringue mixture into a garland, using the smaller pencil circle as a guide. Spread the remaining mixture over the second, larger marked circle to cover it completely. Make the top as smooth as possible. Sprinkle the remaining nuts over the garland of meringue.

4 Place one meringue on its baking sheet on the grid shelf on the floor of the Roasting Oven with the cold plain shelf on the second set of runners for about 3 minutes, or until a very pale cream, then transfer to the centre of the Simmering Oven.

5 Now place the second meringue on the grid shelf on the floor of the Roasting Oven with a new cold plain shelf on the second set of runners for 5 minutes as before, then transfer to the Simmering Oven. Both meringues will need about a further hour or more in the Simmering Oven until firm, turning them round half way through the cooking time. Allow to become cold before removing the baking papers.

6 Place the larger meringue, base side up, on a serving dish. Beat the cream to a soft, floppy consistency and gently fold in the raspberries. Spread most of the filling over the base round and put the smaller meringue, right side up, on top. Fill the 'hole' with the remaining cream and raspberries. Cover and chill until ready to serve. Just before serving, dust with icing sugar. The meringue is best filled about 6 hours before serving.

TO PREPARE AHEAD Wrap the baked, cooled meringue carefully in foil and keep in an airtight container for up to 2 weeks. The finished meringue torte can be kept, covered, in the fridge for up to 8 hours.

TO FREEZE Wrap the finished meringue carefully in clingfilm, then put into a large freezer container to protect it from damage. Freeze for up to 1 month.

TO THAW Remove from the freezer container and thaw overnight in the fridge.

TO COOK IN A CONVENTIONAL OVEN Preheat the oven to 160°C/325°F/Gas mark 3, put the meringue into the oven and immediately lower the temperature to 150°C/300°F/Gas mark 2. Bake the meringue for 1 hour, then turn the oven off and leave in the oven, undisturbed, for a further hour.

CHRISTMAS TARTE AMANDINE

The classic recipe has a layer of apricot jam underneath the almond mixture, but I think the mincemeat gives it a Christmas flavour instead. It freezes well too. Use a bought 500g (18 oz) pack of shortcrust pastry if time is short.

Serves 10

PASTRY BASE
225g (8 oz) plain flour
100g (4 oz) butter, cubed
50g (2 oz) caster sugar
1 egg

ALMOND FILLING
175g (6 oz) butter
175g (6 oz) caster sugar
4 eggs
175g (6 oz) ground almonds
1 teaspoon almond essence
about 225g (8 oz) mincemeat

TOPPING
about 75g (3 oz) icing sugar
juice of $\frac{1}{2}$ lemon
about 50g (2 oz) flaked almonds

1 First make the pastry, either by the usual rubbing-in method by hand or measure the flour and butter into a processor and process until rubbed in. Add the sugar and mix for a moment, then add the egg. Process until the mixture just holds together. Wrap the pastry in clingfilm and chill until firm.

2 Roll the pastry out on a floured surface and use to line a 28cm (11 in) flan tin. There will be ample pastry. Prick the base of the pastry using a fork.

3 Next make the filling – no need to wash up the processor. Process the butter and sugar until creamy, add the eggs and blend, then mix in the ground almonds and essence.

4 Spread a thin layer of mincemeat over the base of the pastry and spoon the almond mixture on top.

5 ⁑ Bake on the floor of the Roasting Oven for about 25 minutes or until golden and firm in the centre. After about 10 minutes, or when it looks a perfect golden, slide the cold plain shelf above on the second set of runners to prevent the tart getting too brown.

⁑⁑ Bake on the floor of the Roasting Oven with the cold plain shelf on the second set of runners for about 30 minutes. When the pastry is golden, transfer to the Baking Oven on the grid shelf on the floor until firm. Cover loosely with foil if necessary to prevent over-browning.

6 To finish the tart, make a glacé icing from the icing sugar and lemon juice, adding water to make it a pouring consistency. Spread over the tart and sprinkle with flaked almonds. Put the tart on a baking sheet and slide on to the grid shelf on the second set of runners in the Roasting Oven for about 5 minutes to give a shiny top and to lightly colour the almonds. Serve warm or cold.

TO PREPARE AHEAD   The pastry-lined flan tin can be kept, covered with clingfilm, in the fridge for up to 12 hours. Filled with the mincemeat and almond filling, it can be kept for about 1 hour, covered and refrigerated.

TO FREEZE   Complete the tart to the end of stage 6. Cool, wrap and freeze for up to 1 month.

TO THAW   Thaw the tart for about 8 hours at room temperature.

TO REHEAT   Loosely cover the tart with foil and reheat in the Roasting Oven on the grid shelf on the floor for about 10 minutes.

TO COOK IN A CONVENTIONAL OVEN   Put a heavy flat baking tray into the oven to preheat. Place the tart on the tray and bake at 190°C/375°F/Gas mark 5 for about 45–50 minutes until the almond filling and pastry are golden brown. Complete stage 6, putting into the oven at the same temperature for about 5 minutes.

TARTE AU CITRON V

If using a metal flan tin with a loose bottom, take great care once the flan tin has been lined with pastry not to push the loose bottom upwards or sideways as it will puncture the pastry. Use a 500g (18 oz) pack of bought shortcrust pastry if time is short.

Serves 10–12

PASTRY BASE	SHARP LEMON FILLING
225g (8 oz) plain flour	9 eggs
100g (4 oz) butter, cut into cubes	300ml (10 fl oz) double cream
50g (2 oz) caster sugar	finely grated rind and juice of 5 large
1 egg	lemons
	375g (13 oz) caster sugar

TO FINISH
a little icing sugar

1 Make the pastry either by hand using the usual rubbing-in method or by machine in a mixer or processor. Measure the flour and butter and mix until it looks like breadcrumbs, add the sugar and mix for a moment, then add the egg and mix well until it holds together. Ideally rest in the fridge for 30 minutes. Use to line a 26cm (10½ in) ceramic flan dish. Prick the base with a fork and freeze for about 30 minutes until hard.

2 To make the filling, beat the eggs in a bowl, add the cream, lemon juice, rind and caster sugar, and mix until smooth. Pour the lemon mixture into the pastry case.

3 ⦂ Bake on the floor of the Roasting Oven, with the cold plain shelf on the second set of runners, for about 30 minutes, watching carefully. Place a greased piece of foil over the tart when the pastry is golden, after about 15 minutes. It may need turning half way through cooking.

⦂⦂ Bake on the floor of the Roasting Oven with the cold plain shelf on the second set of runners for about 30 minutes. When the pastry is pale golden, transfer to the Baking Oven on the grid shelf on the floor until set. Cover with greased foil if necessary to prevent browning.

4 When cool, sieve over a dusting of icing sugar to decorate. Serve with a little single cream.

TO PREPARE AHEAD   Line the tin or dish with pastry about 24 hours ahead, cover with clingfilm and put in the fridge.

TO FREEZE   Best not frozen.

TO COOK IN A CONVENTIONAL OVEN   Bake the pastry blind in a preheated oven at 200°C/400°F/Gas mark 6. Lower the oven temperature to 180°C/350°F/Gas mark 4, pour the filling into the pastry case and bake for about 35–40 minutes until the lemon filling is set. Cover the tart loosely with foil if the pastry begins to brown too much.

A FAT TIP

You can make pastry with butter (or other fat) straight from the freezer. The secret is to grate it straight into the flour. This benefits the pastry doubly – the fat is extremely cold, as well as being in very small pieces.

INDEX